DEEK

The Making of Australia's World Marathon Champion

ROBERT DE **CASTELLA**
with Mike Jenkinson

COLLINS

© Robert de Castella and Mike Jenkinson 1984
First published 1984 by William Collins Pty Ltd, Sydney
Typeset by Post Typesetters, Brisbane
Printed by Globe Press Pty Ltd, Brunswick, Victoria
National Library of Australia
Cataloguing in Publication data:

  De Castella, Robert, 1957–
    Deek.

    ISBN 0 00 217317 4.

    1. De Castella, Robert, 1957- . I. Marathon
    running — Australia — Biography. II. Jenkinson,
    Mike. III. Title.

  796.4'26'0924

Acknowledgments

A World Marathon Champion is a remarkably busy person, but when you can find Rob de Castella he is a frank and generous giver of his information and time. A quick perusal of this book will also show the vital role his wife, Gayelene Clews, played in helping me piece together their story. The idea of such a book was inspired, perhaps unconsciously, by coach Pat Clohessy who has never failed to assist in its progress. In Rotterdam, Pat actually made me feel as if I were contributing something concrete to the de Castella effort. Rob's business manager, Graeme Hannan of International Management Group, always seems to be smiling as he makes hassles vanish and a whole team of expert volunteers helped remove the bugs from the manuscript. They included sub-editor Rob Klima, English teacher Graham Clews and running authority and author Brian Lenton. I have to accept any remaining bugs as my own. Bob Muscat, the General Manager of News Ltd, allowed me to use the company's copy processing computer system to put the chapters together and system experts Dale Mummery and Dave Watkins were unfailingly helpful. During library research for the book I was reminded that Graham Williams of the *Sydney Morning Herald* is one of the most diligent and sharp-minded people in Australian journalism. His 1982 series of articles on Deek was a tremendous help to me, as it will be to future researchers. In the shadow of a deadline, Kay Klima typed the manuscript expertly and even managed some encouraging comments along the way. Terry O'Halloran of *Australian Runner* helped generously with photographs. Libby, Daniel and Hanna were affected in various ways by running mania and put up with me during the project.

THE DE CASTELLA MARATHONS

Year	Event	Location	Place	Time
1979	Victorian championship	Point Cook	First	2:14:44
1979	Australian championship	Herne Hill	First	2:13:23
1980	Olympic selection trial	West Lakes	Second	2:12:24
1980	Olympic Games	Moscow	Tenth	2:14:31
1980	Fukuoka Invitational	Fukuoka	Eighth	2:10:44
1981	Fukuoka Invitational	Fukuoka	First	2:08:18
1982	Commonwealth Games	Brisbane	First	2:09:18
1983	Rotterdam Marathon	Rotterdam	First	2:08:37
1983	IAAF World Championship	Helsinki	First	2:10:03

PERSONAL BESTS

Track		Road	
1,500 m	3:49.8	Five miles	22:52
5,000 m	13:35	15 km	42:47
10,000 m	28:02.7	Ten miles	46:33
20,000 m	58:37.2	Half-marathon	1:01:18
One hour	20,516 m	25 km	1:14:13.6
		Marathon	2:08:18

CHAPTER ONE

'Tree'

Listen to the chat at the starting line of just about any marathon, anywhere.

'What do you reckon you'll do today?'

'Oh, training's been going pretty well but you know how it is. You can never tell until you're out there . . . whether the old biorhythms will be right or not.'

'Yeah, that's right. Part of the attraction isn't it, the uncertainty?'

'I don't know how blokes like Rob de Castella do it. His body seems to be right every time.'

'Beats me!'

In fact, it beats the world. Consistently.

Australia's World Marathon Champion has this to say about the fears that bedevil mortal runners. 'If a person cannot get himself into the best possible shape on a particular day then that reflects either a lack of ability or poor management. It's one thing to have a lot of ability, but it's another thing to be able to utilize it effectively so that you perform at your best in any particular race you choose.'

Once, in Europe, Rob sat on the fringe of a group of athletes bemoaning the fact that the Olympics come along only once every four years. If you weren't at your peak at the right time, they said, you simply missed the boat. The Australian, who had just beaten the American world record holder Alberto Salazar, fidgeted impatiently. Finally he spoke up: 'If you're a top-class athlete it's your business to be right at the right time. You have to manage your preparation and adjust to the timing and conditions of the Games. That's what it's all about.'

Silence followed and you didn't have to be a psychologist to spot the most likely Olympic champion in that Rotterdam hotel lobby. For the achievement of marathon excellence, stripped to its essence, is about mental strength. It's about the will to train, to adapt your own body relentlessly to accept the stresses of running at a seemingly impossible tempo for more than two hours. It's about refusing to answer the twin sirens of weariness and pain when they invite you to spare yourself during the crisis point that comes in every 42.2 km race. It's about single-minded commitment of the kind that has become second nature to Rob de Castella.

The Australian with the gum-tree legs, the heart as tough as ironbark, first unreservedly committed himself to running during an overseas trip in 1979. Not long afterwards he ran his first marathon, winning the Victorian championship in 2:14:44 and since then the 42.2 km road race and its training demands have been the focus of his existence. Many would find his lifestyle onerous and a sacrifice, but Rob has made his choice and is contented with his lot. He comes across as a man at peace with himself and the world.

He says: 'I don't think training in itself is a difficult thing. Running is a natural enough exercise and almost anybody can go out and run. But it's a matter of having the mental discipline to get yourself to do it day in and day out, twice a day, for long periods before you really start to get the benefits. When I started running at school I certainly wasn't thinking forward to World Championships or possible Olympic titles. Or of continuing a training routine for ten years. I always try to take one day at a time. I think if I sat down and thought I might be doing exactly the same things I'm doing now in five or ten years' time — and on every day between now and then — it would be a little bit over-bearing. So I try to take one day at a time and just see what happens. After winning a major race, like the Commonwealth Games, I feel motivated for another 100,000 km. Things like that help a lot.'

The human body is a malleable organism which can be adapted to a surprising degree by the careful, controlled application of stress. Rob and his coach Pat Clohessy have made an investment of twelve years of training, with no more than twenty idle days in that whole time, to gradually adapt the runner's body to accept the stresses placed on it by running 42.2 km at close to three minutes a kilometre. They began with good raw material. Although no running whiz in primary school, Rob inherited a strong physique and a character that is a rare blend of competitiveness and tranquillity from his ancestors who include a Swiss pioneer of the Australian wine industry, Hubert de Castella. Rob's big powerful legs made it possible for him to absorb his training, particularly long runs through the Dandenong hills outside Melbourne, without the minor injuries that plague many young, over-enthusiastic athletes. This genetic advantage, allied with Clohessy's careful management, had a snowballing effect: the more training Rob completed without injury, the stronger he became. The more strength he developed, the less risk he ran of being injured. Soon his durability had earned him the nickname 'Tree'.

Despite his youth he accepted Clohessy's advice to be patient, to progress carefully from one level to another, to wait for the time when his adaptation would be complete and world record-level performances his norm. His mental strength, call it determination if you like but it has many facets, allied with freedom from inner stress or tension made him a remarkable pupil. His wife, Gayelene Clews, explains his personality: 'Robert is a tranquil person, but it would be wrong to label him as placid. That's too negative a word. He can be forceful and can get really angry if he feels it is warranted, but he accepts things. He doesn't fret if, say, the food in Italy or Japan isn't exactly what he requires before a big race. He just believes in accepting situations and making the best of them. We are sometimes late for appointments because he just refuses to let the little things in life ruffle him. I would always be on time but he isn't like that and I found that chacteristic difficult to come to terms with at first. I had meditation lessons in an attempt to match his level of calm. He hasn't studied meditation but he has a remarkable, natural ability to focus his mental energy. He can switch off at will and he can go to sleep anywhere, at any time. He can always sleep on planes and he doesn't worry at all about jet lag. I envy him.'

Millions of TV viewers have remarked on that same calmness as Rob drifted apparently unconcerned through the first two-thirds of an important marathon; they have gasped in admiration as he focused his mental energy over the final third.

He smiles and laughs a lot, has a sense of humour and enjoys company. When the competitive pressures recede, he enjoys an occasional beer and although he is extremely diet conscious he relishes spicy food. But there is no doubt about his priorities. Rob remarks, 'You must have a training routine so that what you do happens automatically. If I got up in the morning and thought about going for a run there would often be a number of possible arguments against it. The thing is to get out and run. Later you can wonder whether you should have or not.'

Gayelene believes that he is single-minded when it comes to training. 'Running has to be the top priority. But he is not closed to other people's ideas or to criticism. He readily accepts criticism from people he respects. He seems to start from the viewpoint that it would not have been offered if it wasn't constructive. Sometimes, when he has allowed side issues to interfere with his main objectives, I point this out. He doesn't become defensive. He just says something like: "You're right Gayelene. I'll have to stop accepting so many invitations."'

Rob's blend of mental and physical gifts, not to mention his years of relentless work, has taken him to the top of the world of marathoning at a time when the sport is more popular and more competitive than at any point in its history. At the end of 1983 he held the world's best mark for an out-and-back course of 2:08:18, only five seconds slower than American Alberto Salazar's overall world best set on a point-to-point course in New York. He was the Commonwealth champion, having won the gold medal in a race described by many as the greatest marathon ever run. He then became *de facto* world champion when he whipped Salazar and the rest of a top-class field in Rotterdam before formalizing his title a few months later with a most impressive victory in the inaugural World Track and Field Championships in Helsinki. He has carefully defined his remaining ambitions in the event: 'I want to become unquestionably the best marathoner ever, so that nobody in his right mind would try to debate that claim. To achieve this I would have to run the best time on record, win the 1984 Olympic title and, in the process, beat all the best marathoners competing at present.'

Asked soon after his World Championship victory to name the rivals still standing between himself and his ambition, he mentioned Salazar at his best and the Japanese Toshihiko Seko, then he trailed off in embarrassment ...

One of Rob's Canberra training partners, author Brian Lenton, asked the world champion to describe himself for his book of interviews, *Through The Tape*. Rob responded, 'I'm quietly confident in my own ability to do things and to achieve what I set my mind to. I don't think it's necessary to come across as a strong or confident person in normal everyday situations.'

Gayelene is a feminist who is far from shy about her views. After a dinner with the couple once, the American Olympic marathoner and gifted journalist Kenny Moore remarked, 'That partnership says a lot about Robert, you know. A man with any insecurities would be uneasy in the company of such a strong woman. He revels in a situation lots of men would be unable to handle. He is so obviously contented and at his ease. It's a pointer to his inner resources.'

Discuss his success with Rob or with anyone who knows him well and Pat Clohessy's name will soon be bouncing around. Rob first came under Clohessy's influence as a 14-year-old schoolboy and twelve years later there is no sign of the relationship wearing thin. Rob says, 'I have as much confidence in Pat as it is possible to have in another person. He has motivated me from the time he took me under his wing at school. He is a very perceptive person and we have a very good understanding of each other. We are very good friends.'

Gayelene offers these insights into the coach–athlete relationship. 'Pat has a lot to offer Robert. Pat no longer plans all the training sessions or attends them all but on occasions when Robert is undecided about something, whether his build-up is right or wrong or whether he should run in this or that marathon, you can be sure he will take the course Pat hints at. He just has so much confidence in him. Pat's not the kind of person to give black and white answers. He will say to Robert, "Well I think you would be better off if you did this" but he will leave the final decision to him. If Pat sensed that Robert had his heart set on taking a different path he would support him and help him make it work out. Often he just helps Robert make up his own mind.

'Robert often makes the point that Pat's coaching with its gradual approach and "train not strain" emphasis would never harm an athlete. Some other coaches, like Percy Cerutty whose approach was very severe, could do great harm to certain runners. But when Pat advises somebody there is always an improvement.'

Clohessy considers one of his major roles to be in reinforcing Rob's confidence before a race. The coach states, 'Everybody needs support and reassurance, even an athlete as mentally strong as Rob. Before the World Championships I told him to have confidence in his finishing power and pointed out that he had sprinted over the top of all three Helsinki 10,000 m medallists in a tight finish in a cross-country race only a few months earlier. His confidence in his finish, which some people believed would be inferior to those of some of the faster track runners in the marathon, won him the gold medal.'

A shrewd man with an unusual insight into human nature, Clohessy has helped mould de Castella the man as well as de Castella the athlete. 'Rob has never been big-headed,' says Clohessy. 'On the way up he always treated other runners with courtesy and was always ready to help. Now that is paying off in the tremendous support he has from the Australian running community. There is very little jealousy or resentment. We have never thought it necessary to hate opponents. That's a destructive attitude and it can backfire. Hate can be a very motivating emotion and it doesn't make sense to go stirring up somebody you're going to race against, does it?'

The two men share a code of conduct that excludes boasting or the making of excuses. It is not easy to extract information from Rob about blisters or other problems he has suffered in a particular marathon. Even Gayelene finds it difficult to persuade him to make predictions about his big events. She explains, 'People ask me what Robert hopes to do in a particular race and I have to say "I don't know". He believes in going out and doing things rather than talking about doing them. He really does not talk about what he is going to do; he doesn't say to me "I can do this today", he doesn't even say "I want to do this today." '

Although he always aims to run within his capacity, de Castella is not impervious to the traumas suffered by lesser marathoners. He has an awkward foot placement which has given him more than his share of blood blisters. He says, 'As I place my foot it twists a little, with a sort of shearing effect as my body passes over it.'

Other deeper effects on his body are being studied by sports scientists and medical experts at the Australian Institute of Sport and elsewhere. As Rob states, 'Some people think running is second nature. Jogging is, but hard running isn't. When you race, you have to concentrate on applying yourself and pushing yourself hard. The temptation is to ease back, because that's what your body automatically wants to do. You have this in-built mechanism which says you should slow down when your body is fatigued. But you can't allow yourself to slow down. What really concerns me is that I shut out all the physiological warning signals during a marathon. My body is telling me to slow down but my mind is able to overcome it. I just cut the signals out. Marathoning is a very punishing sport and not much research has been done on the physiological effects on elite runners. I just wonder how much damage you can do.'

The apparent cold efficiency with which he has executed race plans in big televised marathons has given Rob the image of a kind of sporting hitman. His eyes have been compared by various writers to those of a fighter pilot, a US Marine and a gunslinger, but the real Rob de Castella is an immeasurably warmer person than these media images suggest. One of his great thrills was the realization, after the event, that his victory in the Brisbane Commonwealth Games marathon had made many Australians happy. He felt it a privilege to be able to give pleasure to so many people and a duty to answer the thousands of letters that poured in from adoring children. It was an emotional day for him when he went back to address the pupils of his old school, Xavier College in Melbourne, and they gave him a standing ovation. He told them to commit themselves to whatever they wanted to do in life, to dedicate themselves to doing a good job and to persevere and not give in. Since then he has given priority to speaking engagements which involve children. The birth of his first child, Krista, in late 1983 obviously moved him to an unusual extent.

During the flood of accolades and awards after his Commonwealth Games victory, Rob received a letter from Sydney from the parents of a 14-year-old girl with a grave bone disorder. Little Colleen Kenyon loved jogging because it was the only sporting activity she could manage. She hero-worshipped the Commonwealth champion. Could Rob please send her an autographed picture? The Canberra bio-physicist immediately contacted the organisers of the NSW Sports Star of the Year dinner to be held in Colleen's home city and had her invited. On the night of the glittering presentation he collected the little girl, sat her next to him at the celebrity table and watched over her throughout the evening. She went home wearing the NSW Sports Star medal presented to de Castella and has often been seen in the company of the world's best marathoner on his visits to Sydney since then.

CHAPTER TWO

The Aussie Road

At first glance, Australia looks an unlikely nursery for a world-beating marathon runner. The northern half of the continent suffers weather that makes walking an effort and running only a step away from lunacy. Even in the temperate south, summer temperatures cause tar roads to bubble, eucalypt forests to ignite and would-be sportsmen to conserve their energy in the cool recesses of tiled bars. Just one Australian summer might have been enough to end the careers of many of the fine northern European athletes whose names clog the distance running record books.

Track and field is well down the list of the sports which pre-occupy the nation's fifteen million citizens. It gets scant coverage in the media, surfacing only at Olympics or Commonwealth Games times from beneath masses of words churned out about Australian Rules football, rugby league, cricket and tennis. There was a time in the 1950s when Australian women sprinters were as good as any in the world and such names as Shirley Strickland, Marlene Matthews and Betty Cuthbert were as well known as those of cricket and football celebrities. But it took a modest, curly-headed Melbourne school-teacher, John Landy, and the romance of the quest for the first sub-four minute mile to bring the stamina events to the attention of the masses. Landy lost the globe-spanning race when English medical student Roger Bannister ran 3:59:4 on 6 May 1954. But forty-five days later Landy improved this world record to 3:57:9 and created a

new 1,500 m mark of 3:41:8 along the way. The feats of the Englishman and the Australian made headlines around the world and for the
first time Australians became generally aware, and proud, of a local
endurance runner. More importantly, the nation's distance men
learned it was possible for Australians to achieve performances like
Landy's. It was their first world record. They had not won a single
Olympic medal since Edwin Flack's 800–1,500 m gold double at the
inaugural Games in 1896. Landy's example touched off an upsurge
that made the country, for a period, one of the world's foremost track
powers. The rigorous climate came to be regarded as a conditioning
agent and the image abroad of the Australian track man was that of a
bronzed, weather-hardened, probably crew-cut individual who
overcame the greater finesse of athletes from gentler climes through
rugged strength and unyielding competitiveness.

In 1956, Landy won a bronze medal in the 1,500 m and Allan
Lawrence a bronze in the 10,000 m at the Melbourne Olympics.
During the same year a Melbourne milkman, Dave Stephens, ran six
miles in 27:54:0 to break the world record held by the immortal
Czech, Emil Zatopek. Within three years Australians held world
bests for 1,500 m (Herb Elliott, 3:36:0); the mile (Elliott, 3:54:5); two
miles (Alby Thomas, 8:32) and three miles (Thomas, 13:10:8).

This wave of excellence crested at the Cardiff Empire Games in
1958 when Elliott won the 880 yards and the mile, with compatriot
Merv Lincoln second and Thomas third in the longer event. Thomas
was second to New Zealander Murray Halberg in the three miles and
Dave Power won the six miles and the marathon. At the same time, a
group of Australians headed by Lawrence was competing with
distinction for various colleges in the United States.

At the Rome Olympics in 1960, Elliott, the iron-willed West
Australian who built his strength running up sandhills, won the
1,500 m gold medal and improved his own world record to 3:35.6.
Power ran a valiant third in the 10,000 m after a lonely struggle
against aggressive team tactics by Russian and East German runners.

The 1960s belonged to Ron Clarke, the former world junior mile
record holder, whose training over precipitous forest roads in the
Dandenong Ranges outside Melbourne laid the foundation for
eighteen world records in events ranging from three miles to
20,000 m and an hour. It was a measure of Australians' general
indifference to track and field that Clarke enjoyed greater fame in

Europe than in his homeland where only the *cognoscenti* seemed aware of the way he was revolutionizing standards in the most international of sports. Clarke competed at three Commonwealth Games, winning silver medals for three miles in 1962, for 5,000 m and 10,000 m in 1966 and for 10,000 m in 1970. In Olympic competition he won the 10,000 m bronze medal in 1964 and was foiled by the altitude of Mexico City when he was at his peak in 1968. He finished fifth in the 5,000 m and sixth in the 10,000 m in Mexico's oxygen-thin air, beaten only by runners who had been born at altitude or who had trained at great heights for extended periods. His exertions in those two races left him in a state of collapse and almost certainly began damage to a valve in his heart which had to be repaired with major, crucial surgery thirteen years later.

Clarke was always frustrated by faster finishers in his quest for gold medals, but his records and many victories sealed Australia's reputation as a distance running power. And during his reign there were other triumphs: Trevor Vincent won the Commonwealth Games steeplechase in 1962; Noel Clough the Commonwealth 800 m in 1966; Ralph Doubell the Olympic 800 m in 1968; and in 1970 Tony Manning won the Commonwealth steeplechase while Kerry O'Brien broke the world record for the same event.

In the marathon, a race widely regarded in the 1950s as the preserve of failed track runners and madmen, the national reputation started and ended with a single race . . . Dave Power's gold medal run through the unlovely streets of Cardiff, Wales.

Power, a bank clerk from Wollongong, NSW, was, like Elliott and Thomas, a disciple of the unorthodox, inspirational Victorian coach Percy Cerutty. Then thirty, Power prepared for the 1958 Empire Games running on beaches, sandhills and around a cow paddock. He started in the Cardiff marathon with blank references in the event and appeared flattened by his effort in winning the six miles gold medal five days earlier. In his only other marathon, that year's Australian championship, Power had failed to finish because of severe blisters, a problem that had also bedevilled his track career.

South African Johannes Barnard and Englishman Peter Wilkinson had the times and competitive records to fight out the gold medal contest while Power and his fellow NSW runner John Russell appeared to be among those making up the numbers in a field of twenty-five. No Australian had won any kind of marathon medal at

His eyes have been compared by various writers to those of a fighter pilot, a US Marine and a gunslinger. Deek with an early training partner.

Leaving Xavier College for a training run as a 14-year-old. The moustache was yet to sprout but the legs already had that tree-trunk look.

major games. But Power, a short yet leggy man with a typical Australian crew cut, hid a fighting temperament behind a quiet, self-effacing manner. He said, 'I knew when I won the six miles I would have a good chance in the marathon. I entered the three miles to throw everyone off the scent. When I finished way back (seventh in the best time of his career!) then everyone thought I had no chance and no one was looking for me. That's the way I like it. I prefer to start as the underdog.'

Power took things quietly as the field moved out over a series of hills to the fringe suburb of Rumney. After 15 km his feet began to blister and he was running with pain. But the others could not have suspected his inner struggle as he moved steadily up on the leaders. He remembers, 'I thought of my wife and kids and tried to forget the pain.'

At 16 km, with the race moving into a downhill phase, he pushed himself up to third place. Two kilometres later he passed Barnard to go into the lead. As the road swung along the edge of the Bristol Channel, Power's shoes were squelching with blood but he drove into one of the surges that had broken the field in the six miles (9.5 km). He opened an 80 m break on the South African but ran into another problem: police, race officials and media people were cruising ahead of him in a fleet of cars discharging exhaust fumes straight into his face. Still, he held his advantage over Barnard from the 24 km point until they were within sight of the stadium. The South African, who had built his stamina running in the gruelling 90 km Comrades' Marathon in Natal, then began a brave attempt to run the Australian down. The gap narrowed to 20 m as they entered the stadium and the roar of the crowd poured down on them. By later standards Power was not properly prepared for a fast marathon, but he held off the tough South African to win a magnificent contest in 2:22:45, more than eight minutes faster than the Games record set by another Springbok, Johannes Coleman, back in 1938. Barnard was second in 2:22:57, Wilkinson third in 2:24:42 and Russell came in eleventh.

Medical orderlies caught Power as he collapsed across the finishing line, utterly spent. They were shocked by the state of his feet when they removed his bloody shoes and he had to be carried to the victory rostrum. With the need to keep punishing himself gone, he could no longer bear to put his tattered feet on the ground. A week later, he still could not walk normally.

Two years afterwards, Power made the 10,000 m his main mission at the Rome Olympics. After winning the bronze medal, he toured Europe with a squad of New Zealanders and was greatly impressed by their coach Arthur Lydiard who prescribed heavy mileages but less intensity than the Australian guru Cerutty. Power said, 'Lydiard has achieved great results with his strenuous training methods. It is a tough routine with a long build-up of distance running. He insists that his athletes — even Peter Snell, a half-mile runner — run over the twenty-six mile marathon course at least once a week.'

He began corresponding with Lydiard and bulking up his mileage. It agreed with him. By 1962, when he was approaching thirty-four, Power finished third in the Commonwealth Games selection race and joined the winner Keith Ollerenshaw of NSW and Victorians Ian Sinfield and Rod Bonella, a training partner of Ron Clarke, in the Games team.

Power saw Perth's summer heat as an ally against Games competitors from temperate climates and showed he was not above squeezing a bit of psychological advantage from a patently foolish marathon starting time of 3.40 p.m. when he said 'That time suits me right down to the ground. I don't care if it is hot. I like a bit of heat.'

The six miles was his first, event and he decided to run it aggressively to shake off the fast-finishing Canadian Bruce Kidd. A mile from the finish he threw in a surge that scattered the field but Kidd managed to stay in contact and was too fast over the final lap, winning in 28:26 to 28:34.

Power felt he had made a tactical error by leaving himself with too few reserves at the end of the race, but he over-corrected in the marathon. He and Englishman Brian Kilby ran together to the 30 km mark when Kilby accelerated. Power decided to let him go in the belief he would wilt in the heat. Kilby's spirits lifted as he easily opened a 500 m lead and he was out of sight of the rest of the field for long periods. Power explained, 'I under-estimated Kilby's ability to stay and let him go it alone. But I let him get too far in front and left myself an impossible task.'

Power passed runner after runner as he recovered from a bad spell and chased Kilby home, but he had to settle for his second silver medal of the 1962 Games, while Bonella took the bronze and Ollerenshaw was fourth. It was a disappointment for Power, but a new level

18

of achievement for Australian marathoning with three of the top four placings in a major event.

Clarke dabbled in the marathon, although he seemed somewhat hobbled by his pounding style as well as the suspicions of the long race prevalent at the time. He went through agony in his first attempt at the distance in 1961 and finished in a relatively unpromising 2:53:09. He later wrote: 'Since that marathon early in my career as a distance runner I have run several more and never have been able to get through them without stopping and walking for at least part of the way. It is too demanding a race to be enjoyed frequently, and it seems to be an advantage to be lightly built.'

Clarke, of course, was running before the technological revolution in running shoe manufacture. If he had worn modern, well-cushioned shoes he probably would have found the long race less of an inquisition.

By the time of the Tokyo Olympics in 1964, he was world record holder for 10,000 m and six miles and favourite to win both the 5,000 m and the 10,000 m gold medals. He lost the longer race in a hectic sprint finish in which the American Billy Mills and Tunisian Mohammad Gammoudi proved slightly faster and then blew the 5,000 m through tactical misjudgement. After the second loss he lamented, 'Never before had I felt so depressed about a performance and I was determined to run as hard as possible in the marathon, although, not being a marathon runner, there was no chance of my winning.'

Something less than a lesson in positive thinking!

For most of the marathon he was in third position, but over the final 5 km he dropped almost to a walk as the jarring to his legs became more and more painful. He said, 'An Ethiopian was running so slowly behind me that he couldn't pass me. Several others did and I was grateful to finish ninth in the field of fifty-eight.

Clarke's time was a personal best of 2:20:26 — the fastest yet run by an Australian. The man who didn't believe in himself as a marathoner was leading the way, blazing a trail for a new wave of Australian specialists in the event. However, Clarke was too successful on the track to be tempted by the promise he showed on the road. In addition, the incentive to dabble in the long race was soon reduced by the rise of another great Australian runner.

Derek Clayton was the man who forced the world to acknowledge

Australia as a marathoning nation and his exploits have been both an inspiration and a warning to those who have followed him. Born in Lancashire, England, in 1942, he spent most of his youth in Northern Ireland. When he was eighteen, he watched TV as Herb Elliott demolished the field in the Rome Olympics' 1,500 m. Clayton decided to become a great miler and had cut his time down to 4:27 by 1963 when he migrated to Australia with his family and settled in Melbourne. He joined St Stephens Harriers and within a month found himself running his first marathon, strictly as a training exercise, and clocking 3:00:02. Not long after he realized he lacked the basic speed necessary in the mile (his best 400 m was 52:8 sec) and switched up to the 5,000 m with a vague ambition of running for Australia at the 1966 Commonwealth Games in Jamaica.

In October 1965, he won the Victorian Marathon Club's annual championship in a new Australian record of 2:22:12 and the direction of his athletic life was immediately altered. He prepared for the long run with such intensity that other runners soon learned to avoid training with him. Clarke ran with him once a week, often along the steep roads in the Dandenongs. Clayton recalled, 'I always believed that if you are going to do a 2:08 marathon, you've got to get used to running at five minutes per mile. So I said to myself, "Derek, hammer away at five-minute miles so when you get in a race and you're rested, 4:54 a mile is going to be chicken-feed." And that was my logic. I used to crash it out all the time over as long a distance as possible.'

Clayton had a single ambition which drove him, at times, to run 350 km of intense work in a week and landed him on a surgeon's couch for nine major operations. The intensity of his training created risk; injury was always a possibility as he pushed his body harder and harder in a single-minded campaign to be the best marathoner in history. But he took his chances. He wanted, just once, to run as fast as his body could bear. He said, 'I wanted to get in, reach my potential and get out.'

By 1967 he had improved his PB (personal best) and the Australian record to 2:18:28 and was the national title-holder. But when he went to Japan at year's end for his first international race, the annual Fukuoka International, he was scarcely known outside Australia's comparatively small running community. Most of his countrymen regarded marathoners as closer to circus freaks than national heroes.

In his book, *Running to the Top*, Clayton wrote: 'The best I was hoping for was to get under 2:15, and maybe finish in the top six. It was the first international race I ever ran representing my country. I trained hard for the race, as hard as I could, because I was tremendously proud to be running my first international event. I never considered the possibility of a 2:09. If somebody had asked me at the finish what I had run I would have guessed a 2:12 or 2:13 ... A Japanese official handed me a sheet of paper — on it was written 2:09:36 and I remember thinking, "Well they made a mistake, they left the one off from the front of the nine." I was quite convinced it was 2:19 and not 2:09.'

But the official was right. Clayton had become the first marathoner to run inside 2:12 and he had gone inside 2:11 and 2:10 as well. Morio Shigematsu's two-year-old world record of 2:12:00 was demolished in the process. It was a measure of the distance he was ahead of his time and of the rest of the world, that he was destined to hold the global mark for thirteen years and ten months, despite the best efforts of the world's finest runners, including several talented Americans and their indefatigable publicists.

Clayton wasn't satisfied with being three minutes ahead of the world. He was afraid some fast track man would move up to the marathon and steal his record and reasoned that a time inside 2:08 would be much more secure. He was also driven by frustration when injury foiled his attempt to cement his reputation by winning the 1968 Olympic race in Mexico City. With a huge cyst on his knee, he finished seventh, well behind the Ethiopian winner Mamo Wolde.

After surgery to the knee, Clayton launched into a typically ferocious build-up for a European tour centred on an evening marathon over a fast, flat course in Antwerp, Belgium, in May 1969. He topped off his preparation by winning a marathon in hot weather in Ankara, Turkey, only eleven days before the big event. Such was his attitude to training that he considered this a sharpening exercise.

Antwerp was the night it all came together for Clayton. In a bus taking the runners to the starting line he told Irishman Jim Hogan, 'I'm going for it tonight. I think I can break my world record.'

Hogan looked up, his expression a mixture of dismay and disbelief. 'Jaysus,' he said, 'you're not are you?'

Canadian runner Bob Moore said Clayton was 'as high as a kite' before the race; he had reached an unprecedented peak and was convinced he would beat the record.

The Australian explained later, 'I had a right to be confident, because I knew I was training harder than anyone else in the world. And I knew that — given my day — I could beat anyone in the world.'

He was a big man — 185 cm (6ft 2in. in the old measure) and 73 kg (about 11st. 7lb) — and disagreed thoroughly with the experts who said his physique was unsuited to the marathon. He believed his strong build helped him overcome exhaustion in the late stages of a race, when fast times were won or lost.

The Antwerp race started before 40,000 spectators waiting for the kick-off of a soccer game. It was a cold, still night and Clayton shivered with anticipation as he started his warm-up. Moore led from the gun and took them through 5 km in 14:58 before the Australian, with his crooked, head-wobbling style, strode into the lead. He went through 10 km in 30:06 and the halfway, all alone, in 1:03:55. He said, 'Crowds lining the course were shouting at me. I was grateful for this gauntlet of humanity. They were taking my mind off the pain of the run.'

Buoyed by the crowd and the sense of speed that comes with running at night he felt strong and well until around the 27 km mark. He describes the rest of the race as a nightmare. He couldn't understand the splits shouted at him in Flemish-accented English and drowned by the whistling and shouting of the spectators. Fatigue mounted and he felt sure he had fallen off the pace and squandered the chance of a lifetime. 'Those last 10 km blended together in a nightmare of horns, shouts, bicycles, exhaustion, pain and fear ... I began to retch violently, bringing up bile that gagged me as I breathed.'

The sight of the stadium lights lifted him over the final kilometres and in the bedlam of the finish he heard somebody shout: 'Two, oh eight ...'

He had done it! A new world best of 2:08:33.6. But the price was to be high. He had pushed his body beyond its limitations and he would never run nearly as well again. He was urinating blood, vomiting black mucus and passing black diarrhoea. And there was lingering fear, because no doctor could explain exactly what he had done to himself. It took him six months to recover his health and although he chased marathon excellence and games gold medals for another five years, success eluded him. 'I thrashed myself,' he said. 'The pain in my legs and gut was excruciating. I had pain in my kidneys and bowel ... I know that I reached the maximum.'

Clayton retired in 1974 after being forced to pull out of the Christchurch Commonwealth Games marathon with a groin muscle injury. But his courage and his record lived on as a challenge to the elite.

The other outstanding Australian marathoner of the Clayton period also started life in the Old World. John Farrington was born at Moreton-on-Marsh, England, in 1942. Unlike Clayton, he was a noted performer in his native country, reaching the status of junior cross-country international before joining the great swell of post-war emigration to the southern continent. Involvement with the marathon began in Australia in 1967 while he was working as an administration officer at Sydney's Macquarie University. He achieved enough immediate success to be chosen as Clayton's understudy for the Mexico City Olympics in 1968 but a foot injury and other factors kept him down to a modest forty-third placing.

Farrington returned home determined to train himself to the levels of the world's elite. He had no coach but quickly won respect as a shrewd self-conditioner. In 1969, a year in which he soaked up heavy mileages, his best time was 2:21:22 but the following year he improved by more than eight minutes to 2:12:58 and also won his first Australian title. Through the first half of the 1970s he continued performing at international standard, although he was often in Clayton's shadow and persistently worried by foot injuries. Steady improvement was testimony to his intelligent training program: 2:12:58 in 1970; 2:12:14 in 1971; 2:12:00 in 1972 and 2:11:13 to win the NSW title at Richmond in 1973, a performance that was the fastest in the world that year and made him the seventh fastest in history. That was a vintage year for Australia with Clayton's 2:12:07 making him third best in the world and three others, Brenton Norman (2:14:33), John Birmingham (2:17:23) and Peter Bruce (2:18:46), all bettering 2:20. There was not to be a better display of national depth until 1978 when seven men ducked inside 2:20.

In 1975 Farrington equalled one of Clayton's feats by winning his fourth Australian title at Point Cook, Victoria. The surprise of that race was a young Tasmanian, Dave Chettle, who led for all but the last 100 m. It was Farrington's fourteenth run inside 2:20 but he confessed to a waning of enthusiasm. 'I find it hard now to push myself to fast times. I've lost much of my interest in the marathon. But I'm still aiming for a place in the (1976) Olympic Games team and will keep going until then.'

Farrington missed the Games, but he didn't stop running. In 1978, at thirty-six years of age, he won a marathon in Adelaide in 2:25:25.

His best performance at a major Games was his fifth behind England's Ian Thompson at the Commonwealth meeting in Christchurch in 1974 when he clocked 2:14:04. Throughout his career he raced widely and helped Clayton create an image of Australia as a marathoning nation. In four of the seven years from 1967 to 1973, the fastest marathoner in the world was an Australian.

The retirement of these two — and of Clarke — from top competition left something of a vacuum. Young Melbourne runners Bill Scott and Chris Wardlaw and Adelaide 5,000 m man David Fitzsimons battled to plug the gaps on the track, while Chettle, the Tasmanian who built his strength running up Hobart's Mount Wellington once a week, achieved a Clayton-like breakthrough in his first major international, the Fukuoka race in 1975. Chettle went to Japan encouraged by his coach's prediction that he was 'ready to run a 2:14' and after a duel with Canada's Jerome Drayton, one of the big names in the sport, finished a close second in 2:10:20 to become the second fastest Australian. His subsequent career had as many peaks and gullies as the rugged west coast of his home island, and he had the misfortune to produce his best post-Fukuoka effort on a mismeasured course.

In 1978 Queenslander Gerard Barrett, in a desperate bid for Commonwealth Games selection, ran 2:12:20 and a year later Scott and Wardlaw crossed the Fukuoka finishing line in fifth place with their hands joined to force the judges to tie them. Their twin marks of 2:11:55 removed any statistical doubt about Australia's standing in the event. The national reputation, which once had rested on Power's one race, could now call as evidence the deeds and times of Clayton, Chettle, Farrington, Barrett, Scott, Wardlaw and many others. There was a tradition for young runners to follow and a wealth of experience on which they could draw.

CHAPTER THREE

The Clohessy Creed

The exploits of Landy and the world-class performers who followed him had galvanised the Australian running scene in the mid-1950s when a skinny kid from Muswellbrook began winning New South Wales country titles. Pat Clohessy emerged from his small-town, Catholic school background into the wider world of top-class competition during a most exciting period for his home State. Allan Lawrence, Albert Thomas and Dave Power led a distance-running group which matched most in the world for quality in depth. When Clohessy moved to Tamworth, Lawrence recruited him for Randwick–Botany club and persuaded him to commute to Sydney (a 900 km round trip) to compete at weekends. The young runner found himself in a tough but stimulating environment. It wasn't long before he was racing with the best of them over the dark grey, crumbly cinders of the E. S. Marks Field. One of his clubmates at that time, all-rounder Peter Bowman who was later to become Administrator of the Australian Institute of Sport, recalls, 'I can remember his early races against the established runners. He would go three lanes wide most of the way but he wouldn't let go. You don't often see such raw talent and guts.'

Landy coached Clohessy by letter and there was more immediate help to hand, as Clohessy recalls: 'Runners like Lawrence, Thomas and Power were a tremendous help with advice and encouragement, even though I was knocking them off sometimes.'

Like many other young runners, he saw harder and harder training sessions as a short-cut to success and did not always follow the advice of Landy or the others. 'I got carried away, with consequent loss of form.'

Following a routine of track repetitions in the fashion set for the rest of the world by Emil Zatopek, he took some fearful hammerings in training. This appeared to pay off before the 1956 Olympics when he beat Power in a NSW three-mile record of 13:48, the second fastest run by an Australian. Success, like a siren, beckoned from the other side of even fiercer repetition sessions. He increased his workload and broke down. 'Over-training led to my loss of opportunity when I think I was competitive against the best, particularly at 5,000 m.'

Lawrence collected a 10,000 m bronze medal at the Melbourne Games and Thomas finished fifth in the 5,000 m, while Clohessy nursed his injuries and considered himself the victim of bad luck. The next season Clohessy ran a one mile PB of 4:04 behind Thomas and got carried away again. He built up his 400 repetitions to the point where he once ran forty in a session. After that he was so flattened he could manage only 4:17 for a mile.

The correspondence with Landy continued and Clohessy absorbed some of the Victorian's late-career wisdom. 'The complete unselfishness of Landy motivated me to help other runners,' Clohessy said later.

The late 1950s were a time of decision for elite Australian runners. Athletic scholarships were available in increasing numbers in the United States and could be used to gain a degree and ensure a post-competitive future. But departure to the US had to be weighed against the chance to run for Australia at the Empire Games in Cardiff, Wales, in 1958 — an ambition as natural to Australians as the dream of Olympic competition. Often, the deciding factor was whether the runner was academically inclined or not. Thomas stayed in Australia and won a mile bronze medal and a three-mile silver medal in Cardiff and set his two world records in Dublin. Power stayed, too, and won his gold medals for six miles and the marathon. After being run out of a place by Elliott, Merv Lincoln and Thomas in the Australian mile title, Clohessy opted for a history course at the University of Houston in Texas where he had the company of fellow-Aussies Lawrence, Barrie Almond, Geoff Walker and later Laurie

Elliott, younger brother of the great miler.

Initially, Clohessy did well in cross-country but was frustrated on the track. He remembers, 'I was training well but I think I was so tired I wasn't absorbing it. We were racing four or five times a week, doubling on occasions and this combined with a heavy repetition diet had a flattening effect. On some occasions we did 20 x 400 and on others 8 x 800.'

Here were the seeds of two of the key tenets of the creed Clohessy later developed about the right way to approach distance running. The first principle holds that the training workload must be increased very gradually so the runner can absorb it comfortably; the second concerns an athlete's *total environment*. To progress properly he must not be under undue strain in study or the workplace. His future must be secure enough to ensure he is free from stress and his personal relationships should, ideally, be tranquil. Sleep and rest should counter-balance training output.

For Clohessy in his freshman year at Houston, the total environment was far from stress-free. He was a diligent and, in the end, highly successful scholar and the cares of the classroom piled upon the cares of the training track and the competitive arena. With the advantage of hindsight, he said, 'As well as training, you need adequate rest, relative relaxation in your job or study; if you are working or studying too hard or intensively or working very long hours in a demanding job and not getting adequate rest, this has a big influence on what you can absorb in training. I'm very aware of that in the light of my own experiences. I made a lot of mistakes in that area and I am very sensitive about it. If you err, it is better to err on the side of under-training and be relatively rested and fresh as compared to over-trained. If you are over-trained you run the risk of being injured, as with myself. It cost me a lot.'

Clohessy was so dedicated and talented (he once won the 100 yards in 10.3, the 220, 440, 880 and mile in a single afternoon at a Muswellbrook sports day) that not even the multiple pressures of American college life could keep him down. In his second year at Houston he was runner-up in the National Collegiate Athletic Association three miles and he won the title for the next two years, 1961 and 1962. He won All-American honours at three miles and in cross-country and set Texas collegiate records for the mile (4:04.1), two miles (8:47.8) and three miles (13:26).

When he decided to spend part of the 1961 summer vacation racing in Europe, the experience transformed his athletic life. He linked up with a group of New Zealand runners touring under the guidance of the brilliant coach Arthur Lydiard. The party included Olympic 5,000 m champion Murray Halberg, Olympic marathon bronze medallist Barry Magee, Olympic 800 m champion Peter Snell and a promising 800 m man, Gary Philpott. The Kiwis knew their way around the European circuit, having toured there after their Games triumphs in 1960. Clohessy found their company uplifting. 'Just travelling and competing with them, learning that they were only human, helped my confidence. They also impressed on me the necessity of doing long runs in pre-season training.'

The 1960 Olympic successes of the black-vested runners from tiny New Zealand amazed the world but widespread acceptance of the ideas of Lydiard, the 100-miles-a-week man, was still well in the future. Lydiard revolutionized running in New Zealand with his insistence on the value of near-marathon mileages, even for those specialising in events as short as 800 m. Snell's success at the Rome Olympics spoke for itself, and it had been backed up on the same day by Halberg's triumph. Clohessy's eyes widened as he saw the way the New Zealanders trained and the results they achieved. Lydiard stressed relaxation and was a master at building a runner's confidence. His methods had to be better than 40 x 400 m and a 4:17 mile.

As if in gratitude for this deliverance from drudgery, Clohessy took over the pacing duties while Halberg attacked two Australian-held world records. At Jvaskyla in Finland Clohessy did the early work until the wiry New Zealander lit out on his own to run consecutive miles in 4:15 each and take two seconds from Thomas' world two-mile mark. Clohessy reduced his own best from 8:48 to 8:41 and Lydiard greeted this improvement as further vindication of his methods.

The next big race was a 5,000 m in Stockholm. The Australian led for the first six laps, going through the one and a half mile point in 6:35, a pace faster than he had ever dreamed possible. Eventually he faltered and Halberg and Magee swept past on the strength of their marathoners' training mileage. It was a two-man race until the last lap when Halberg unwound a withering sprint to break Thomas' three-mile record with a time of 13:10 and to get within 0.2 second of

Vladimir Kuts' 13:35 record for 5,000 m. Clohessy clocked 13:56 and said: 'I died in the later stages, but it was still satisfying to play a role in Murray's record.'

Back at Houston the Australian propagated his new training gospel. He, Elliott and Almond measured out 42 km along the shoulder of Highway 90 while high-speed American traffic whizzed past. Clohessy ran the full distance twice and the results of his efforts showed in the following season. He ran an aggressive 5,000 m against Magee in the Coliseum Relays in Los Angeles, only to be edged out in the final few metres. Peter Snell, who ran at the same meeting, described Magee's escape from defeat as 'miraculous'. Snell wrote in his book *No Bugles, No Drums*: 'With 220 yards to go Pat Clohessy shot past him and, by the home straight, had a race-winning lead of ten yards. It looked all over when, sensationally, Pat faltered with 50 yards to go. Barry, still unable to step up his pace but still not losing any, was incredibly able to sneak past and win in the relays record time of 14:10:2.'

A few weeks later, in the 1962 NCAA three-miler run in the hot-house of Eugene, Oregon, Clohessy trailed local hero Dale Story until the final circuit and then unleashed a 56.3 lap to win by 50 m. He also won the one and three miles at the Kansas Relays and the two miles at the Drake Relays. Clohessy said: 'My racing improved because I was much fresher. I'd just do something like 6 x 200 m easily because we were racing regularly. I was racing more consistently because I wasn't over-trained. Off the track I'd just do easy ten-milers.'

Better form won him selection to contest the Commonwealth Games three miles in Perth. He finished seventh in a tough, tactical race in which Halberg outsmarted the young Canadian Bruce Kidd and Ron Clarke made his international breakthrough to win the silver medal. In the US in 1962, Clohessy was beaten only once over a mile and lost only a single event over a longer distance, the 5,000 m at the Compton Invitational when he battled Halberg right to the tape. Clohessy beat Kidd for second place and regarded the race as one of the best efforts of his career. And, as in the previous year, he bounced back from defeat, this time to win the AAU three miles — a considerable feat at the time because American distance runners were beginning the surge that would win gold medals in both long track events at the Tokyo Olympics. Clohessy was not discouraged.

'The experience of having good wins in consecutive years at national championships after defeats by the New Zealanders made me aware that a beating can be good for an athlete. Sometimes you need a defeat to bring out your best.'

Clohessy's *total environment* also improved when he graduated *cum laude* with a major in history and a minor in economics. A Houston newspaper columnist, John Hollis, wrote at the time: 'Patrick Andrew Clohessy is one of those men who make you feel like the product of a misspent youth. He runs five miles before breakfast, likes to study, reads history books for a hobby and eats oatmeal. He holds all the University of Houston track records and carried a history major and economics minor through four years as easily as he swings through a four-mile practice jog.'

The university paid Clohessy one of its highest compliments, presenting him with the Charles Saunders Award given annually to the graduate who has shown superior leadership, scholarship and athletic achievement during his four-year course.

That summer Clohessy ran for Australia at the World Games in Scandinavia, collecting a bronze medal over 5,000 m behind the Englishman Bruce Tulloh and France's Michel Bernard.

Moving from Houston to Austin to study for a masters degree in history at the University of Texas, Clohessy immediately became a guiding influence among that college's younger runners. In December 1963 he raced over the marathon distance for the first time. The value of his new training was placed beyond question when he won in 2:22:19, a time faster than Power's winning effort in Cardiff and bettered only by Keith Ollerenshaw among Australians. During a trip to Sao Paulo, Brazil, for the annual Round-the-Houses race he was approached by a US Marines runner, Billy Mills, for training advice. Impressed by the potential of the part-Southern Sioux, Clohessy talked him into modifying his system of repetition workouts to include longer, more relaxed running and hill work. When Mills amazed the world a few months later by beating Australia's world record holder (and Clohessy's friend) Ron Clarke in the Tokyo Olympics 10,000 m, the die was cast. Clohessy's future would be involved in helping other runners achieve excellence.

The nature of the advice he would later give was further reinforced by bitter experience. The 1964 Games were likely to be his last chance to represent Australia at an Olympic meeting. Once again injury frustrated his hopes when he strained a hip muscle. Unable to string together the sort of 5,000 m performances that would make the selectors back in Australia sit up and take notice, he hoped for a while that his marathon effort would earn him a ticket to Tokyo. It did not turn out that way.

Back in Australia with two degrees, Clohessy studied for his diploma of education and began teaching and formal athletics coaching after appointment to Oakleigh High School in the suburbs of Melbourne. He moved to Xavier College as a history teacher and later house master and found the circumstances ideal for developing cross-country as a mass participation sport, with the emphasis on recreation and enjoyment. The best of the school's cross-country group usually found their way into the track team and were encouraged to progress gradually, without pressure or over-intensive training. The long-term result was that many Xavier students stayed in the sport after leaving school and became the nucleus of a Clohessy group training in the Dandenongs and at various venues around Melbourne. When they were joined by such talented outsiders as Chris Wardlaw, Tasmanian Dave Chettle, Stephen Foley and, occasionally, Bill Scott, the situation became a fertile one for a Melbourne-based running renaissance, with the Clohessy creed as its guidelines.

The creed, of course, took many years to evolve and the process hasn't ended yet. Unlike many other coaches Clohessy is, by nature, a listener as well as a talker and as interested in hearing others' ideas and experiences as in broadcasting his own conclusions. His theories are most strongly influenced by Landy, Lydiard and Derek Clayton.

Landy taught him to use the Australian environment as a conditioning tool and made him aware that speed could be built just as effectively on a hilly bush trail as on the artificial, geometric conformity of a 400 m track. Clohessy said, 'John Landy began running in the mountains when he was assigned to Timber Top School, the annex of Geelong Grammar which Prince Charles later attended for a period. Landy modified his training, which had been influenced by Emil Zatopek, from intensive track repetitions to include longer runs and short, fast work over the hills. He was always considered to lack finishing speed but corrected that to such an extent that he came down and almost beat the American 880 yards world record-holder Lon Spurrier over his own distance. He showed that the hills were crucial to developing strength and that running long distances could actually improve your speed. Before Landy's time our runners were very aware of Australia's isolation and they felt somewhat inferior to the Europeans who produced most of the records, won most of the gold medals and came up with all the new training ideas. Landy's excellence broke this feeling of inferiority. His world mile record in Finland in 1954 was very important for Australia. On a personal level he helped countless runners with advice and counselling and I get a lot of satisfaction from the feeling that I am carrying on his work.'

Lydiard totally converted Clohessy the runner and has had a continuing influence on Clohessy the coach. 'Lydiard influenced me greatly in the value of longer work, run relatively quickly. It increases your speed, your balance and your efficiency. Rob de Castella was ungainly and awkward, but continual long running forced him to become more efficient. Lydiard's system is based on periodization, with his runners spending a certain period on long, slow work, then doing hill work, then track work and finally racing. We've modified that to suit Australian conditions where we have opportunities to race throughout the year. Aside from the big marathons, there is the club track season, the State and national titles, cross-country, road racing and fun runs. Because of this we have adopted a system of complex conditioning where the various stages of Lydiard's program are fitted into each week's work.

'We train similarly the whole year round, only modifying our workouts to prepare for specific events. We do our long work at a relaxed pace, but go hard on the hills. The courses at Ferny Creek in the Dandenongs have some very difficult hills and these are tackled hard. We stress easy running and insist on lots of recovery running after hard workouts. We do fast work on a hill circuit in a park. And when I say fast, I mean it. They belt up those hills flat-stick. We do track work once a week, which adds variety to the program and provides a useful yardstick to the athletes' progress. If you do the long work and the hill work, which is run very fast, you can produce your best on the track at short notice. It's a functional system which allows you to run well all the year round.'

The influence of the third man, Clayton, on the Clohessy creed was almost totally negative. Although the coach has the greatest admiration for the courage of the runner who held the world

Gayelene offers congratulations after Rob's Australian Marathon Championship win in Perth in 1979 while Pat Clohessy seems intent on taking him away from all that.

Sweet victory. Rob, 22, wins his first senior international track race, the Pan Pacific Conference Games 10,000 m in Canberra in 1979.

Rob beats some great American heroes to win a 15 km event on the US circuit in 1981 but Superman (at left) doesn't seem at all distressed by the eclipse of his fellows. American races seldom lack colour.

marathon record for nearly fourteen years, he emphasized the difference in the approach of his athletes in these words from 1981. 'We don't regard a few isolated great runs as fulfilling. We don't want to run world records and miss out in the big competitions. We aim to reach a plateau where we can run at world record levels and keep on doing it. We've only touched on it yet. To reach these levels you have to be patient and to temper your training and that's what Derek taught us. He used to tear around at five minute-a-mile tempo in training and concedes now that he over-trained and was his own worst enemy. I used to visit him at Christmas when he went into hospital for annual surgical repairs to his legs. Injuries cost him training time and then he would be even more impatient when he returned. We've got to practise restraint so we don't fall into the same trap.'

Clohessy's system, as applied to his most famous pupil, evolved slowly along with Rob's increasing ability to absorb bigger work-loads. A typical week in 1983 would have gone like this:

MONDAY

7 a.m.	10 km in about 38 minutes;
Noon	About 30 minutes of gymnasium work: flexibility and strengthening exercises;
5.15 p.m.	16 km in an hour;
10.30 p.m.	Sleep. (Ideally, this is routine seven nights a week.)

TUESDAY

7 a.m.	10 km in about 38 minutes;
Noon	30 minutes in the gym;
5.15 p.m.	10 km in 38 minutes followed by twelve laps on a grass track, sprinting the straights and jogging the bends. About 1,600 m jog to warm down.

WEDNESDAY

7 a.m.	10 km in about 38 minutes;
Noon	30 minutes in the gym;
5.15 p.m.	About 29 km in approximately 1 hr 50 min., mainly on soft pine-needle trails in the Stromlo Forest.

THURSDAY

7 a.m.	10 km in about 38 minutes;
Noon	Weight training and circuits;

| 5.15 p.m. | 5 km in about 18 min, followed by 8 x 400 m clocking about 63-4 each. De Castella sprints each 400 m lap and then floats for 200 m. Another 5 km in about 20 minutes. |

FRIDAY
7 a.m.	10 km in about 30 minutes;
Noon	Weight training and circuits;
5.15 p.m.	About 18 km in approximately 64:45.

SATURDAY
| 9 a.m. | 19-21 km in about 18 minutes/5 km pace followed by 6 x 100 m sprinting up a hill; |
| 5 p.m. | 10 km in about 38 minutes. |

SUNDAY
| 9 a.m. | 33-6 km in 2 hr 15 min. to 2 hr 40 min.; |
| 5 p.m. | 8 km in about 31 minutes. |

Clohessy usually uses the word *advise* rather than *coach* when he talks about his relationship with runners. John Andrews, a Sydney town planner, came under his influence during Australia's 1981 cross-country tour of Europe and the track team's visit there in 1982. After beating de Castella in the Emil Zatopek 10,000 m in December 1982, Andrews remarked, 'Pat set training programmes and generally had a good look at me. One point he made was that I should incorporate more steady runs in my training. I guess I used to over-train. I just didn't know when to stop. He also told me not to train when I had injuries. I'd had quite a few in the past and some of them kept me out for six months at a time. By taking his advice I have had no injuries for nine months and it has been my best year.'

Brisbane runner Gerard Barrett echoed Andrews' theme in a literately elegant article in the *Age* late in 1982. He began his career as a teenaged disciple of the eccentric Victorian, Percy Cerutty, and believed every training session had to end in exhaustion — purity through pain. His marvellous promise (10,000 m in 27:50.7 and a marathon in 2:11:42) remained unfulfilled, the victim of repeated interruptions through injury. He confessed to a Pauline conversion to the gentler ways of Clohessy. He wrote (with abridgement):

'In 500 B.C. a Greek philosopher, Heraclitus, wrote: "A man can never step in the same river twice. The man is different, and so is the river."

'Over a period of (injury strewn) years it has become apparent to me that most injuries are not the result of bad luck. Each has a cause, and by and large it is up to the individual to fix it. This means changing things to eliminate errors and deficiencies in the training programme.

'The greatest mistake a runner can make (and I am not alone here) is to plot the shortest possible path back from injury to full training. This approach leads only to increased down time with injury and a resulting slow progression in fitness. Moderation is the key to being on the track and racing.

'Naturally to speak with such zeal I must be a convert. Pat Clohessy, the National Distance Coach, has been quietly guiding Rob de Castella on these lines since Rob was a teenager, with obvious results. My own training has been evolving slowly in this direction with each injury. But it has now become more moderate than ever to match my most serious injury to date.

'A river can change a lot in a year, so too can the man who steps into it. If he wants to.'

Like all good teachers, Clohessy could earn the respect of even the most reluctant pupils. He could also exert authority, although he is a gentle, softly-spoken man who seems able to find time for anybody needing his advice. When you talk about him with runners, among whom he is a growing legend, it doesn't take long for the anecdote to surface about the 5,000 m man who tried to set a PB (personal best) in a club race but pulled out after only 3,000 m. According to the story, Clohessy rushed over to him, patted him on the back and said, 'That's one of the best first halves of a 5,000 I've seen run on this track!'

The coach laughs that story off as apocryphal, but the generations of Xavier College boys he schooled in cross-country remember his encouraging claps on the shoulder, whether they finished first or 51st. 'It's a matter of building up self-confidence and self-image, no matter what your level is,' he insists. 'Everybody needs encouragement. The more support they get, the more motivated they become to do better. It's a matter of encouraging potential and they take a lot of persuading before they become aware of how good they can be.'

This optimism about his runners is sometimes quite disarming and he admits to weaknesses in his charges only with obvious regret. He was appointed to the new post of National Distance Coach in 1979 and left Xavier on extended leave at the end of 1982 to take up a coaching appointment at the National Institute of Sport in Canberra. In his early fifties, Pat Clohessy is still as lean and wiry as he was when he first started to take on the top runners at the E. S. Marks Fields thirty years ago. He has no interest in veterans' competition ('What have I got to prove?') but runs regularly with his charges and plays a handy game of tennis.

Running is a lifetime commitment. Clohessy expects his athletes to be patient enough to wait for long-term benefits from their programmes. 'Through regular training they will be able to absorb more and more work as they go along. Temperament and perseverance are important. They have to accept a philosophy of gradual physical adaptation without over-training and running the risk of the kinds of injuries that plagued Clayton and limited my own performances.'

A runner's competitive career is comparatively short and often it is over before he recognizes his own mistakes. As a dedicated teacher, Clohessy is determined the wisdom of hard experience, the Clohessy creed, should be available to the new generations, so the same mistakes won't recur in a barren unproductive cycle.

It would be a fortunate young runner who opened his mind to Pat Clohessy's guidance.

CHAPTER FOUR

First Steps

Just an easy hour's jog from Clohessy's home in bayside Brighton, lies the comfortable middle-class Melbourne suburb of Kew. As you walk up the hill in Barkers Road, you come to a large house with bay windows overlooking a shady garden with liquid amber, Japanese maple and other trees. It's a well set-up home with ample hints that a large family lives there: the cars, the belongings in the living areas and the volume of washing, with running gear draped on the lines even on non-laundry days. Rolet and Anne de Castella have lived at no. 315 for more than twenty years and their seven children have grown up there. It is a warm, lived-in place, lively but relaxed. Just the sort of home in which you could prepare yourself for a long, hard journey.

Anne and Rolet, both in their late fifties, are devout Catholics. She is a nursing supervisor at a nearby private hospital, resuming her family-interrupted career so the children could have costly private education. A fine tennis player, Anne takes to the court as often as her other commitments permit. Rolet is an executive with the Nestles food empire and some of the running gear on the back line is his. He has the boiled-down, greyhound look of a veteran marathoner and has completed around twenty of the 42.2 km races since he suffered a heart attack at the age of fifty-one. For a year he couldn't walk up stairs without severe angina pains. Doctors told him it was probable that a congenital intolerance of fats had been one of the causes of the attack. Rolet then began a study of diet which has made him, in the words of his family, 'a nutrition fanatic'. A follower of Dr Nathan Pritikin of the Longevity Centre in California, he has given up red meat, salt and fats, believing quite firmly that what he eats and drinks is a matter of life and death. He also believes in the health-inducing qualities of running. He ran and dieted his way out of convalescence after his heart attack, gradually building his mileage up to an occasional peak of 220 km a week. His first marathon after his heart attack was a 3:36 and he subsequently joined the twelve per cent of runners who have broken the three-hour barrier with a 2:58:48 effort in 1980, an outstanding run for a man of fifty-six. Naturally his experiences have had an impact on his children, especially on his eldest, Robert, whom Rolet first coaxed into joining him for early morning runs when he was twelve. Rolet recalls, 'He was running in school races and coming nowhere. He hated being dragged out at seven in the morning, but he had a sense of humour. He made a thing out of finding short cuts so he could beat the old man home. After a while he didn't need the short cuts. He was motivated by his running and began to improve.'

Rob was a somewhat ungainly, poorly co-ordinated boy who met little success in the traditional Melbourne sports of Australian Rules football and cricket. He was attending Burke Hall, the preparatory school for the expensive, Jesuit-run Xavier College, and became involved in their cross-country programme. He would finish fortieth or fiftieth in a field of 150 and Anne de Castella remembers the time he came home absolutely jubilant because he had improved to thirty-sixth.

The boy's fun-loving approach to his new sport reflected both his personality and home environment. 'He's always had a relaxed and happy nature,' his mother says. 'He was pretty exuberant as a boy. He worked hard at school but he didn't shine academically.'

She was the daughter of an army man and, possibly because of that, didn't believe in too much discipline in the home. 'I couldn't have survived with seven children unless it had been a relaxed atmosphere. We only ever had one rule in this household. That was that if you started something you didn't quit it. You committed yourself and you did your best.'

At the age of fourteen Rob left Burke Hall to join Form Three at Xavier and to come under the lasting influence of Clohessy, the school's track and cross-country coach. Their partnership was an accident of history that was to be felt from Boston to Addis Ababa.

Clohessy wrote in the late 1970s in Mike Agostini's *Australasian Track and Field* magazine about his protégé's early years: 'Rob (otherwise known as DeCas) was an inconspicuous competitor in cross-country at Burke Hall before coming to Xavier. He developed quietly as a schoolboy with early promise evident in cross-country where he showed considerable strength, much persistence, ample confidence and a fine group spirit from which he got more motivation and interest than from any personal pressure to excel. In any case he refused to acknowledge pressure even then; cross-country was fun, an interest, a hobby. His parents encouraged Rob's excellent attitude which allowed him to develop quietly. He moved into an unusual environment where schools' cross-country was emerging as a relatively popular team sport at Xavier and, indeed, at many private schools involved in a weekly competition. At fourteen Rob was a game competitor indeed and usually placed in the first ten.'

This relaxed approach did not inhibit improvement; nor did the first tastes of success dampen Rob's sense of fun. He had a strong feeling of mateship and Clohessy recalls a time when he finished well ahead of the field in an inter-house race and then ran back to piggyback a teammate who was running second. He had hoped to eliminate any loss of points suffered by his beaten mate, by forcing the judges to declare them equal first. Sadly, the adults were not amused and disqualified both boys. On another occasion he turned up pale and with rings under his eyes for an inter-school event and Clohessy learned he had been out until 3 a.m. trying to find his way home after being led blindfold into thick bush in a Boy Scout prank. The coach was furious. 'I told him if he ever did that again, he'd be out of the school team. He never did that sort of thing again on the eve of an important race.'

Rob told Brian Lenton in *Through The Tape* how an inconsequential accident influenced his running development at this early stage. 'There was one cross-country race where I lost a shoe in the muddy conditions and I was so mad that I went really hard. I easily started picking up places and finally finished twelfth or thirteenth, which was my highest placing ever. It made me realize that you get somewhere with aggressive running.'

The early promise was there. At fifteen, the lad shot into second place in both the Victorian All Schools cross-country event for his age group and in the 1,500 m on the track. It was time for Clohessy to introduce him to the famous Ferny Creek circuit in the Dandenongs. Rob started on comparatively short 20 km forest runs but soon joined the senior athletes over distances up to 34 km, including the formidable hill of more than 3 km known as the Ron Clarke Hill. The youngster treated the outings as a social event rather than training. Sharing ice blocks at the finish was the day's highlight. He was still only fifteen when Tim O'Shaughnessy, the national junior 1,500 m champion, complained to Clohessy, 'The young buck is becoming a nuisance racing up the hills.'

The coach recalled, 'I noted that remark with satisfaction, curiosity and expectation.'

Rob was competing regularly and also running over a 16 km course once a week with his schoolmates. He developed into a formidable cross-country racer, logging up thirty consecutive victories from 1973 to 1975, including a front-running triumph over another rising star, Gerard Barrett of Queensland, for the national junior title in 1975. Progress on the track was slower and he was often out-sprinted by faster boys at the end of races. But in 1973 the breakthrough came with a fighting victory in the Associated Public Schools 3,000 m and a win in the All Schools under-17 3,000 m in an Australian record time of 8:35.4. A year later he scored a memorable double by clocking another national 3,000 m mark, 8:20.4, and then ran a personal best of 3:57 for 1,500 m only ninety minutes later.

Eighty kilometres training each week, strong physique, stress-free attitude and love of racing had moulded him into an outstanding prospect by his final year at Xavier. The 17-year-old and Clohessy produced a blitz on the Australian junior record book, with times of 13:58.4 (5,000 m), 13:31 (three miles), 29:11.8 (10,000 m), 28:15 (six miles) and finally 8:49 to erase a long-standing two mile record set by Herb Elliott. Selected for his first overseas trip to the New Zealand Games in Christchurch, he won the schoolboys' 5,000 m.

There was speculation that Rob would run at the Montreal Olympics in 1976, two years later, but he showed extraordinary maturity for his age when he told a reporter, 'When you start worrying about the future and whether your times are good enough or that you are making enough progress it ceases being fun and becomes a job or real drudge. I just want to enjoy running and the satisfaction it gives me. Pat Clohessy is my history master at school and his guidance is probably the reason for any success I may have had. Before the race [his 5,000 m record] he told me what tactics to use because I had never run the distance before and had little idea how to pace myself... I love running and all I want out of competing is the personal enjoyment I get.'

Clohessy's response was cautious optimism. 'He has great potential and would easily compare with the top-liners of his own age overseas. I have been training him for about four years and his temperament and attitude to competition and training are his great assets. If he continues to improve and can get overseas experience, he could easily represent Australia.'

CHAPTER FIVE

Dandenong Days

Clohessy saw the young runner's first three years out of school as the 'consolidation stage'. In his first year in the adult world, 1976, Rob was fortunate to train regularly with Chris Wardlaw, then getting into shape to make the final of the 10,000 m at the Montreal Olympics. Wardlaw continually reminded him that schoolboy stars, particularly those from expensive private schools, often lost interest when they bumped their noses against the hard reality of open competition. This good natured banter only thinly disguised a concern that such ability should not be wasted. Wardlaw, the little fellow with an artist's beard and a guardsman's ramrod back, was a vital ingredient in the mixture of personalities that created a distance-running revival in Melbourne in the 1970s. He was nick-named 'Rabbit' or 'Rab' and Ron Clarke once wrote, not without affection, that the name was due more to his bouncy personality than to his rather prominent teeth. His running achievements were con-siderable: representation at two Olympics, PB's of 28:15.6 (10,000 m) and 2:11:55 (marathon), victories in Sydney's City-to-Surf and San Francisco's Bay-to-Breakers and numerous fine national and international road and cross-country efforts. Yet he played an even more important role as a catalyst in the development of other runners. His infectious high spirits, encouragement, leadership, training example and, later, athletics journalism helped many along the road to success. Clohessy did not coach him, but the two were close friends. Wardlaw said, 'Pat advises me, but he coaches Deek. There's quite a difference. It's a matter of personalities. I couldn't imagine actually being coached by Pat but it seems an ideal arrangement for Deek.'

Clohessy clearly saw the benefits to the young de Castella. 'The group headed by Wardlaw was a very important factor in Rob's development. If it's used properly, the group is a very motivational institution as far as training goes. It helped Rob tremendously in the vital years after school. It makes training more disciplined in that you have to turn up at a time that suits others. And it's more than just the training. You're exchanging ideas and chatting away and it's much more relaxing. You can get a lot of work done and it's not anywhere near as hard or intensive as when you are on your own.'

Another factor favoured Rob and other runners of the new generation, as Wardlaw pointed out. 'They joined the group and accepted the levels of performance we had battled for years to achieve as the norm. In the early 1970s Bill Scott had gone out, almost on his own, in pursuit of excellence. Then there was Dave Fitzsimons in Adelaide, Graeme Crouch, myself and others working to bring our times down to international standards. The new runners were in a better psychological situation because they saw no barriers to the levels we had struggled to reach.'

Clohessy's supervision and Wardlaw's company helped maintain Rob's enthusiasm through the potentially distracting post-school years. It wasn't always easy. Clohessy explained it this way: 'Like a lot of youngsters just out of school, Rob developed a taste for parties. He stayed out late and didn't make it to some training sessions and I was advised to tell him to shape up or ship out. But I was aware of his potential and rode out the storm. It was just part of growing up. There are a lot of inflexible coaches about with no athletes to coach.'

Rob recalls that his racing form fluctuated sharply during this period as he continued to train but sometimes missed out on the rest needed to complement the hard work. Running for pleasure and satisfaction, rather than in any single-minded quest for excellence, he still managed a share of successes, usually placing well in the many road, cross-country and fun run events he entered. He notched a notable victory in Sydney's hotly contested 14 km City-to-Surf in 1977, setting a course record, and not long after won his first senior Australian cross-country title and selection in a national team to compete in the IAAF Cross-country Championships in Dusseldorf, West Germany. This was an important event for the young athlete and for Australian distance running generally. The IAAF race, also known as the World Cross-country, was held every year, usually in Europe, and featured fields of more than 200 runners with quality in depth unmatched in any other event, even an Olympic 10,000 m. The cross-country race attracted Europe's and America's best in events ranging from 800 m to the marathon. High placings were desperately hard to achieve and a continuing exposure of an Australian team to this kind of competition was certain to have an impact on local standards. Clohessy and other far-sighted officials hoped to ensure Australian participation every second year, giving new interest to the years between Commonwealth and Olympic meetings.

Australia had first competed in Rabat, Morocco, in 1975, placing eleventh as New Zealand became the first nation in the event's eighteen year history to break a monopoly on the teams gold medal shared by England and Belgium. The Australian placings were Bill Scott 2nd; Jim Langford 42nd; Chris Wardlaw 48th; Rob McDonald 49th; Dennis Nee 116th; Dave Chettle 128th; and Rob Talay 149th.

They needed to do a bit better two years later in Dusseldorf to convince the AAU that the exercise was worth the expense. In the individual races, Leon Schots (Belgium) beat Carlos Lopes (Portugal) by five seconds and Belgium edged out perennial rival England 126 points to 129 to secure the team honours. But the Australians placed a respectable sixth behind Belgium, England, the Soviet Union, West Germany and New Zealand, with the best performances coming from Steven Austin, 15th; Wardlaw, 23rd; and Gerard Barrett, 34th. De Castella, 20, was 37th and ahead of scores of runners with bigger reputations.

Having broken the international ice he plunged in with enthusiasm, placing 11th in the West German cross-country championships, 4th in a race in Belgium and then 16th in the classic Italian event, the Cinque Mulini, which is run every year in the countryside near Milan and attracts high-quality fields. The runners weave their way around and, in some cases, through several antique mills, racing all the way between crowds of excited fans. A placing in the top twenty is always an achievement and young de Castella returned home well-satisfied with his first visit to Europe, the home of cross-country.

Back in the Dandenongs and at other runners' gatherings, the talk was all of rising Australian standards and the need to train consistently to match the best European performers. Dave Chettle left Tasmania to join the Clohessy group and found Rob an enthusiastic partner for his long runs. The quality of their work was emphasized that November when Chettle beat an immensely strong field in the Auckland Marathon only to find the course had been mismeasured. His time of 2:02:24, just one second ahead of Italian Franco Fava, would have translated into his second sub-2:11, at least.

Wardlaw continued to goad and cajole the members of the group to raise their ambitions and improve their performances. Clohessy commented, 'Rob gained interest, motivation and experience through working closely with Chris and the others on the long runs at Ferny. Ken Hall trained with them before going to Europe in 1979 and running his 3:55 mile, and Max Little was particularly helpful.'

Rob, it seemed, just couldn't find enough training partners. 'Sometimes I went over to Bill Scott's place and we ran from there. He didn't train with us regularly but I found him good company and he gave me a lot of encouragement. Despite his achievements and his nickname in Melbourne of the "Living Legend" he is the sort of relaxed, easy-going person who I feel most at home with.'

Training was always a social experience. Rob's brother Nick joined the party when his architectural studies permitted, as did Marcus Clarke, Ron Clarke's son, and Greg McMahon, a promising youngster also involved with books. The tall, stylish middle-distance runner Stephen Foley was a regular, and Barrett made one or more visits from Queensland each year.

Clohessy wrote at the time: 'Robert credits his enjoyment of the sport, facilitating his development, to all this group activity. And I totally agree with him. Who could run 1,000 days straight without this group interest? Another significant influence: Rob's mother Anne is a champion tennis player and his father recently ran a 3:18 marathon ... Rob has inherited an admirable competitive temperament with the accent on perseverance and relaxation — and absence of pressure. This, above all, has enabled him to negotiate successfully his various stages of development.'

Clohessy pointed out that the senior de Castellas had always encouraged Rob to enjoy his running and had told him to give it away if it ever become a chore. They successfully walked the parental tightrope by motivating him, without putting him under undue pressure.

The 1978 track season saw Rob score a significant 10,000 m track victory over the fancied American Greg Fredericks at the Pacific Conference Games in Canberra. But it was a year in which distance runners were given a raw deal by the national selectors when they chose a team for the Commonwealth Games in Edmonton, Canada. Gerard Barrett was particularly unlucky to miss out after clocking 27:51.4 for 10,000 m and 2:12:20 for the marathon. So the frustrated runners turned their minds to the IAAF cross-country race to be run in Limerick, Ireland, the following March. Rob assured himself of a place in the team by chasing Wardlaw home for fifth place in the selection trial. The trip to Europe became a decisive passage in his life, of the kind described in Shakespeare's *Julius Caesar*:

'There is a tide in the affairs of men,
Which, taken at the flood, leads on to fortune;
Omitted, all the voyage of their life
Is bound in shallows and in miseries.'

If Rob, then 22, had missed this tide, his life may not have wallowed in 'shallows and in miseries' and it would probably have been easier, but it would have been less rich in adventure and achievement.

The Australian men's team was managed by Clohessy and made up of Rob, Scott, Wardlaw, Barrett, Steve Austin, Chettle, Rob McDonald, Jim Langford and Bryan Lewry. But more important, as far as Rob's destiny was concerned, was the fact that two women were to join the squad to run as individuals to gain experience. He already knew Lyn Williams and Gayelene Clews casually through encounters at athletic meetings and training camps. Gayelene, now 18, had approached him for an autograph when he had run second to South Australian Tony Bart in the national junior cross-country race in Perth in 1974. She recalls, 'I went up with my little brother and Robert signed an autograph for me. I've still got it somewhere. After that we occasionally exchanged a few words at national titles over the years. We both won national cross-country titles in 1978 when I was 17 and he was 21. I gave him a congratulatory kiss and that was the first time we had a real conversation. He had long hair and a full beard and I thought he was rather a scrappy person. He looked a bit like Charles Manson. Then, when we assembled at Melbourne airport to fly to Ireland, he turned up with his beard shaved off and his hair trimmed. I thought "Oh gee, he's not bad looking under all that." I was rather amazed.'

The dark-eyed West Australian came from a clan of formidable runners in Perth and was regarded as a very game competitor. She had represented Australia previously in an annual 10 km road race for women in Puerto Rico. She told Rob she regarded running as an art form, an almost total expression of one's self. He jogged with her, he listened, he talked. Gayelene said, 'I found that I really enjoyed talking to him and being in his company. My mother's first impression of him was that he was a good, sincere listener. In a conversation he really pays attention to what you have to say and will spend time digesting your ideas. He doesn't keep silent out of politeness while he is waiting to get in a word. He measures up what you are telling him. He doesn't interrupt or interject and he doesn't like other people doing that. I suppose, initially, that was what I liked most about him.'

The two young runners found themselves in each other's company more and more often. Wardlaw took to warning Rob he would be better off doing more training and less 'lying around' but Rob and Gayelene laughed and made a tentative date to go to a disco together on the night after the big race.

Then, almost before he knew it, he was on Limerick's Greenpark racecourse running with 220 other athletes from twenty-five nations through mud above his ankles. It was a five-lap event over 12 km and as local hero John Treacy took the lead in the third lap, crowd control broke down and the runners' right-of-way became narrower and narrower. People dashed across the track to get a better view from the inside as Treacy glided ahead of the mud-splattered field to successfully defend the title he had won the previous year in equally muddy Glasgow. The Australians ploughed along together, bunched in the middle of the field. Although they all finished strongly, only Barrett and Austin could manage decisive forward moves. Austin led them home in 29th place followed by Barrett (32nd), Scott (36th), Langford (40th), Lewry (45th), McDonald (51st), de Castella (62nd), Wardlaw (72nd) and Chettle (102nd). The team placed sixth behind England, Ireland, the Soviet Union, West Germany and Belgium.

It was, of course, a great day for the Irish. One newspaper

described Treacy's breasting of the tape as: 'A moment frozen in the minds of those privileged to witness it and destined to be recalled for generations yet unborn.'

But Rob was shocked. An obscure sixty-second place just didn't fit his self-image at all. Gayelene had finished fifty-first in the women's race and the Irish visit marked the beginning of chronic knee problems that were to plague her for years. As was her way, she told him frankly that he should have run better. He was reading the biography of Brendan Foster, the great English track man who had fought tooth-and-nail with the best of them over distances from 1,500 m to 10,000 m and was known everywhere for his guts on the track and his friendliness off it. Foster's book emphasized the importance of hard work and its paramouncy over simple talent. One sentence about commitment kept recurring in the mind of the young Australian: 'All top international athletes wake up in the morning feeling tired and go to bed feeling very tired.'

Weariness wasn't a problem that night as Rob turned up at Gayelene's door for the long-awaited date. She was mildly surprised he had remembered their casually made arrangement, but said to herself, 'Oh well, fair enough,' and took his arm. They were still dancing when all the other Australians had wandered off to bed.

The team moved from misty, soggy Ireland to the crisp, clear weather of northern Italy and Rob moved a long way towards a new level of achievement. His mental attitude hardened, despite Wardlaw's contrary suggestions and teasing about the youngsters' blossoming relationship. Gayelene realized they were growing closer. 'In Milan we became aware that we enjoyed each other's company to an unusual extent. We managed to be together a great deal of the time, on buses, having something to eat, at training. Our romance actually had a bit of help from the Kenyan runners Samson Kimobwa and Henry Rono. Henry kept insisting I go to a disco with him, while Samson actually suggested I go back with him to Africa to become his fourth wife. I was only eighteen and they really made me feel uneasy. When we got on a bus to go to training or somewhere else, they would jostle to get the seat next to me, so I began telling them I was keeping the seat for my Australian boyfriend. When Robert arrived he would ask, "Is this seat for me?"'

'I would reply, "It certainly is. Sit right down!"'

'The Kenyans helped make us inseparable.'

For 30 minutes of each weekday Rob uses the Australian Institute of Sport's superb facilities to improve his muscular power and flexibility.

At home in the Stromlo Forest, Canberra, where the training foundation was laid for triumphs at Brisbane, Rotterdam and Helsinki. It is possible to run 35 km in the forest without covering the same trail twice.

Leaving the Institute of Sport in Canberra for a lunchtime run along nearby bush tracks.

The field for the Cinque Mulini was one of the best ever assembled, with four European champions over various distances, three of the fastest five 10,000 m runners in history and fourteen sub-13:30 5,000 m men. Rob moved up with the in-form Barrett and Scott to battle it out with the big names. He was unrecognizable as the middle-of-the-field plodder of a few days previously in Limerick. In the end Barrett stole some of his glory by finishing fourth but Rob came in eighth, just losing a three-way sprint finish with the brilliant Englishmen Mike McLeod and Steve Ovett. He was ahead of the Finnish European 10,000 m champion Martti Vainio and Kimobwa, the world 10,000 m record holder. He had been competitive with the best in the world and was able to tell Wardlaw, who placed 13th, 'It looks as if there are hidden benefits in lying around!'

After the race, Clohessy took the youngster aside and said, 'This is what you can do if you discipline yourself, if you want it badly enough. If you really want to succeed, you have the ability. The rest is up to you.'

There was no longer any fear that Rob would miss the tide. He was ready to commit himself, mind, body and soul to his running. He asked Clohessy to map out a new training programme including two runs every day, a much higher total mileage and more sleep. The coach felt Rob's background of consistent training would enable him to absorb the extra work without the risk of injury and drew up a new routine.

The Australian squad decided to see a film together on their last night in Milan, so Rob knocked on Gayelene's door. She wasn't sure she wanted to spend her last night in Europe at a movie and by the time she had agreed to go along, the rest of the party had already vanished. Left to their own resources, the young couple bought gelati and strolled hand-in-hand past the wondrous Gothic cathedral with its white marble facade and 135 spires and across the Piazza della Scala with its famous opera house and fringe of outdoor restaurants. It was a mild, moonlit evening and courting couples were passing to and fro. There was magic in the present, but parting was close and the Australians' conversation drifted towards the future. He had a girlfriend in Melbourne and she a boyfriend in Perth. Perhaps their feelings for each other had been artificially intensified by the glamour of a sporting tour and the romance of Europe. Gayelene said, 'We thought our feelings would probably change when we were back home and settled into a more mundane way of life. We talked about writing letters but decided it would be better not to endanger two established relationships. A clean break seemed the best idea but as soon as I was back in Perth I became upset because he didn't write. I thought, "This is really hopeless" and when I had some photographs from the trip printed that gave me an excuse to send him a letter.'

Rob's return letter contained the sentence: 'I think, if we ever had enough time together, we could grow to love one another.'

Meanwhile, Clohessy who had remained overseas for a month after the Cinque Mulini, returned to Melbourne to be told by Wardlaw: 'You'll have to talk to Deek. He's been racing too much in training.'

Others in the group confirmed that Rob was working harder than they had seen him do before and running them off their feet.

Clohessy said jubilantly, 'This is the sign. He's going to make it!'

Rob was as attentive to his correspondence as he was to his training. He exchanged letters with Gayelene for eighteen weeks until he went to Perth for the Australian marathon championship. On the morning after that race the two of them rose at 4 a.m. It was to be their last day together for many weeks and they wanted it to be as long as possible. Gayelene remembers that day vividly. 'We went walking around the city, talking and window shopping, and bought a newspaper which had his photo on the front and back pages. Then we drove to King's Park, the beautiful park overlooking the city, and watched the sunrise. We drove home to have breakfast with my parents and announced that we were going to be married.'

It was a long-distance engagement, with Gayelene in Perth and Rob in Melbourne for most of the year. Fortunately, the national cross-country titles and the national 25 km road race were also run in Perth that year, so the struggling science student was able to pay his fiancée three visits without having to meet the expense of trans-continental flights. Problems apart from geography arose when the traditional Catholicism of the de Castella family collided with Gayelene's ardent feminism.

'We planned to be married by a female celebrant in an outdoor ceremony at an old colonial homestead near Perth,' she explained. 'We didn't believe the church had much to contribute to what we thought marriage should be about. Robert had grown away from Catholicism before we met but I remember hearing him talk with his father on the telephone: "No Dad. It isn't just Gayelene. Dad . . . I haven't been to church for years . . . No Dad, Gayelene doesn't have everything to do with that . . ." That sort of thing.

'Robert no longer believes all the dogma associated with Catholicism. He says he likes to think of himself simply as a Christian. I don't agree with the Catholic Church at all. It has a very oppressive attitude towards women.

'We wrote our own marriage vows and were married in a beautiful garden at the homestead, almost in the paddocks with the sheep. It was just what we had wanted.'

Despite these differences, Rob's parents made the arduous drive across the Nullarbor Plain to be at the ceremony and all his family who could afford the trip were there.

The newly-weds lived for a while in Perth before moving to Melbourne where, for a time, the couple became a trio as American Sue Schneider, whom Gayelene had befriended in Perth, moved in with them. Gayelene said, 'When Sue arrived in Melbourne she didn't know anybody, so we suggested she come and live with us. I had met her in Perth in 1980 and helped develop her interest in running. Before that she was just a generally fit person who played squash, rowed and took part in fun runs occasionally. Through being with us she became involved in athletics and proved so talented she finished fourth in the national cross-country trials in 1979 and ran second in the Australian 3,000 m track championship. She was fun to live with and became Robert's second closest female friend. He loved teasing her about her accent. When she returned to America in the middle of 1981 she quickly made a name for herself in road running, finishing ahead of people like Laurie Binder and Jacqueline Gareau on occasions. Some acquaintances were surprised that a newly married couple could share their house with somebody else but it was never a worry to us.'

But then the Clews–de Castella partnership was never a terribly conventional one. Journalist Graham Williams of the *Sydney Morning Herald* wrote after interviewing them in 1982: 'They are a rare couple. They have an almost symbiotic relationship. They openly kiss, cuddle and embrace each other, although she has retained her maiden surname because she does not want to lose her individuality. She understands completely Robert's all-consuming passion to become, as he puts it, "not only the best, but unquestionably the best marathon runner in the world".'

Rob appreciates his wife. As he said, 'She has provided me with a lot of motivation, particularly with the way she has struggled against her knee problems. Gayelene is terrific, too, in the way she has given me support and encouragement. She realizes I have to withdraw into myself before a big race, that I get self-indulgent and self-centred. But she's always a great support, especially when things aren't going so well. When things are going well it's easy to train but when I'm not racing well I need support and motivation. Everybody who is associated with me has to be positive all the time. I can't afford for them to be negative. It takes a special kind of person to live with that.'

The relationship works, so obviously it is not all one-way. Rob takes his turn with the household chores and in preparing meals, accepts only those social invitations which include Gayelene and she travels overseas with him whenever it is possible.

Does she resent his running being the pivot in their lives? 'No. If I was achieving the performances Robert is, I would expect our lives to revolve around me.'

The Clews/de Castella partnership was a major improvement in the runner's 'total environment'. She would be involved, to some degree, in all his future successes. He would often comment that his last really disastrous race was in Limerick, just before the start of their romance.

CHAPTER SIX

Snow Gums and Black Snakes

Rob hadn't been long out of school when he first enrolled in one of distance running's toughest higher educational courses: the annual athletic pilgrimage to Falls Creek in the Australian Alps. Melbourne runners had been trekking to the northern Victorian ski resort every Boxing Day for almost fifteen years. For these few weeks they enjoyed uninterrupted training in a communal, mutually motivating atmosphere at elevations up to 1,986 m above sea level — almost as high as you can go in Australia without wings. This annual session of intensive conditioning on mountain roads and walking tracks was a natural extension of the traditional long Sunday run in the Dandenongs. It was launched in the early 1960s as a reaction to the sudden successes of runners from the highlands of Africa. There were constant arguments, which continue still, about the extent to which the Ethiopian, Kenyan and Tanzanian successes were due to genetic factors or to the results of training at high altitude. But there was general agreement that a low-altitude athlete could improve his capacity to utilize available oxygen by training in the mountains. This belief was accompanied by widespread disagreement on the degree of this improvement and the length of time it would continue to benefit the runner after he returned to sea level. Such arguments became part of the social life at Falls Creek in December–January every year and although elevations in the ancient, weather-worn Australian continent were paltry compared with those of such places as Addis Ababa (2,370 m) and Mexico City (2,230 m), the runners agreed that three or four weeks in the mountains left them fitter and tougher.

Falls Creek perches at the top of the spectacular Kiewa Valley, just below Mount Bogong, Victoria's highest peak. Most visitors go to the resort in winter when it is glamorized by a carpet of snow but in summer it shows a few raw edges; discarded building materials and rubble fringe many of the new ski lodges. In the ski season it becomes a swirl of frenetic, fast-spending activity but in high summer there are only bush walkers, runners and the background music of birds and cicadas.

Driving up to the village you pass through tall ferny, eucalypt forests and you may have to brake at night for grey kangaroos, euros and an occasional wombat. But the resort is close to the tree line where even the hardiest snow gums show the pressures of life in temperatures ranging from 30°C to –22°C and where the monthly mean remains below freezing for two-thirds of the year. At the edge of their range, the white snow gums bend their attractive green and brown-blotched limbs close to the ground as if cowering before the fierce winds that buffet them throughout the year. Above the tree line are the heathlands and alpine moors of the Bogong High Plains, a region of many faces. It is buried under deep snow in winter, gaudy with wildflowers in spring and dark and forbidding when storm clouds glower in summer. The cries of little ravens are morbid sound effects and the occasional stretches of water can be as melancholy as Scottish tarns. People react to it in various ways. South Australian 5,000 m man Dave Fitzsimons went home after two days, appalled by the grimness of the greyish heath, the lack of tree cover and the treachery of the footing on the rock-strewn walking tracks. Nick de Castella, a student of architecture as well as an outstanding runner, had a different opinion. 'When it's misty I like the soft greys, the muted colours. Then, when the sun's on it, it's transformed . . . it's really something.'

The comparative coolness of the High Plains in summer attracted an annual migration countless years before the runners began their visits. The area is named from an Aboriginal word for a type of moth, greyish-black and about four cm across the wings, which pupates in the lowlands at the beginning of summer and migrates to the Australian Alps to shelter from the heat in caves and crevices at 1,500 m or higher. The insects mass in layer upon layer in suitable places, surviving the summer on fat stored in their bodies and then dispersing back to the lowlands in autumn. The highest mountains shelter the densest clusters of these Bogong moths and the Aborigines once scaled the heights every year to feast on their protein-rich bodies. They would singe away the wings in a fire, then pound the bodies into a nutritious paste. This easily secured food provided an unusual opportunity for a gathering of large numbers of people in one place for social and ceremonial inter-action. Early European settlers described the Aborigines as going into the mountains lean and hungry and returning fat and sleek.

The modern, athletic pilgrims aim for an opposite physical effect. When Rob first joined their itinerant community in a block of holiday apartments designed for skiers, Clohessy and Wardlaw were the central figures in a floating population of about thirty athletes and their families. Most of the faces were well-known to the youngster from his sessions in the Dandenongs and other venues around Melbourne, but there were occasional visitors from other parts of Australia and even New Zealand. The life was communal and single-mindedly athletic. The occupants of different apartments took turns to provide the one heavy meal of the day, in the evening. Breakfast and lunch were makeshift affairs left up to individual tastes and habits. Runs of various distances, alone or with companions of varying standards, were available every morning and every afternoon with the hours in between usually spent in luxurious inactivity, watching sport on TV, napping, talking running with Clohessy, gossiping or competing in endless sports trivia quizzes in which Wardlaw and marathoner Len Johnson vied for the honour of asking (and being able to answer) the most esoteric questions. Plato observed a long time ago that athletes in training were sleepy creatures and Falls Creek in early afternoon would do no harm to his thesis.

But when the time came for action it was torrid. The morning run was often 30 km or longer, over steep unpaved mountain roads and bush tracks where a twisted ankle or snapped toe could be instant punishment for waning concentration. The longer runs usually started at a comfortable pace but it was difficult to keep a thin edge of competitiveness from creeping in before the end. There were occasional injuries, and this caused some coaches and athletes to doubt the wisdom of training in such a risky environment. But Rob said, 'I think they are over-cautious. There is a slight risk, but we feel it is more than compensated for by the benefits. The constant strain of running on uneven surfaces, the twisting and adjusting, strengthens your joints, especially the ankles, and gives tremendous leg power. It's a type of conditioning you cannot get on a track or flat road.'

The afternoon sessions would usually be easier recovery runs, possibly 13 km over a moderately undulating gravel road around Rocky Valley Dam above the village or a jaunt along one of the four-wheel drive tracks built to give access to the ski field's drainage aqueducts. These tracks had a gentle gradient but were crossed every few hundred metres by concrete spillways which were easy to jump into but increasingly tiresome to scramble out of as a run wore on. A stranger, unused to the thin air and the pace, even of a recovery run, could find himself slipping into oxygen debt and beginning, in that condition, to hate the grey and red gang-gang cockatoos which screeched at him from the shrubbery in rasping Jimmy Durante accents.

Rob was soon as at home in the mountains as the ubiquitous and beautiful crimson rosellas and often competed with Wardlaw ('I'm just keeping the youngsters honest these days') and Barrett to lead in the procession at the end of the long runs. Over the evening meal — usually great heaps of plain food, such as chicken and steamed vegetables or a baked dinner — he would join in — planning more and more ambitious runs. One especially testing climb, to the summit of a peak called Spion Kopje, had become a weekly training feature. When this lost its element of adventure, an extended trek was devised starting with a climb up the Staircase Track to the summit of Mount Bogong, continuing across the relatively gentle contours of the High Plain but then plunging into an extremely steep descent to Big River and climbing again along Duane Spur. Johnson recalled, 'We often talked in comfort about runs like that but we very rarely did them.'

One time they actually ran the course. It took almost an hour just to reach the summit of Bogong and further muscle-numbing hours to begin the climb at Duane Spur which was so steep the members of the party who elected to walk found themselves gaining on those who were still running! Sue Schneider won Rob's total respect by

going the whole distance. Although she was often behind the
different stages of the run, she always came plodding patiently
the main group, sometimes carrying posies of wild flowers she
been unable to pass. As they waited, Wardlaw would tell the other
'Sue will never make it. I knew she shouldn't have come.'

Then when she appeared he would be so relieved he would shout,
'I knew you could do it, Sue. These other blokes reckoned you would
get lost.'

The whole journey took five hours and ten minutes and ended,
according to Johnson, in 'aching quads, dust, dirt and sheer
exhilaration'. Rob was convinced by Sue Schneider's performance
that she had the capability to make a big impression in distance
running if she chose to take it seriously. After training like that, why
would she or the others be afraid of a marathon?

The High Plains are a notoriously unpredictable environment.
Storms race like breakers up the Kiewa Valley and blizzards have
been known to trap walkers in the middle of summer. Lightly dressed
athletes are aware of this and it is a powerful incentive to keep on the
move, even when quadriceps begin to quiver and lungs to burn.
Copperheads and red-bellied black snakes are common along the
high waterways and most of the runners, at some time or other, have
swerved around or even hurdled snakes basking in the sun. Such
experiences, no doubt, help improve the ability to accelerate during
racing.

Gayelene said of the pilgrimages, 'They were a time of intense
effort but they were also very relaxing. We would often spend a whole
afternoon putting together a huge jigsaw puzzle or doing something
else that you would never find time to do at home. It was always a real
holiday, in spite of the mileage the uninjured ones would absorb. We
would sometimes drive up at night to one of the peaks and just lie
down on our backs and watch the stars which seemed so big and
bright in the clear, thin air.'

Clohessy also put great store in the annual spells at Falls Creek. He
believed the chance to train twice a day with ample rest in between,
the motivation gained from being constantly with a group of
dedicated runners and the physical and mental toughening effect of
the environment played an important part in Rob's progress from
former top junior and promising young international to potential
world champion.

Chapter Seven

Marathon Apprentice

It would have been easy to miss Rob's emergence as a prospective world beater on a fine, cool August morning at Herne Hill near Perth in 1979. Along the 30 km to 35 km stretch of this Australian marathon championship course he first showed the awesome late-race power he could bring to bear on a 42.2 km event. Following a 25 km to 30 km split of 16:07 he suddenly kicked down the pace to 14:50 to rip the heart out of his opposition and sound an ominous warning to other aspiring marathon champions.

That Australian title was the second stage of his apprenticeship to the long run. The debut took place a few months earlier at Point Cook near Melbourne, when he entered the Victorian title after an encouraging series of cross-country, road and track performances following his return from Europe. He had scored twelve wins from twelve starts. Clohessy was convinced he had stepped up to a higher plateau of athletic development and was prepared for the character-testing event for which he had seemed destined even in his school days. Rob was ready. 'Things were going well and Pat and I began to look ahead to the 1980 Olympics. The marathon seemed the event in which I could make the most impact and we realized I would have to get a couple under my belt before the Australian selection trial. I was a bit apprehensive about the Point Cook race. I didn't want to destroy myself. I had heard all the bad stories. About the Wall and about runners wiping themselves out for the rest of their careers. So I was a bit cautious and ran comfortably early. Very comfortably, in fact.'

58

A previous national champion, Vic Anderson, opened an early break while Rob tagged on to a bunch of experienced marathoners and followed Clohessy's exhortations to relax and enjoy himself. In spite of his caution he was only fifteen seconds from the front at the halfway and as Anderson weakened in the second half the young colt ran precociously into the lead. Rob said, 'I was well within myself even when I started to pick up the pace a bit after halfway. Pat and I had decided that I would run easily for the first 30 km and then, if I was feeling good, I would run on strongly. At 32 km I said to Pat, who was in a car, that I felt like picking it up. Every mile after that was faster than the preceding one.'

He looked strong and comfortable as he moved away from Anderson, David Byrnes and Paul O'Hare to cover the final 10.2 km in 30:55 for a race time of 2:14:44, the fastest first-up marathon by an Australian. Arriving home, he was still fresh enough for his third run of the day and wrote a daily aggregate of 57 km into his training log. The results of the championship showed two R. de Castellas — Rolet, 55, ran the course in 3:25:14 as an early step in his post-heart attack campaign to better three hours.

Clohessy went to Perth with Rob for his attack on the national title, to be contested over a flat two-lap course at Herne Hill. It was a happy coincidence for the young runner that the race was in the distant west and ended, temporarily, his separation from Gayelene.

At the start, conditions were calm and the temperature 8 degrees, but it rose to 22 degrees during the second half of the race. Clohessy and Gayelene cruised along beside the runners in a car with the coach advising 'take it easy' and Rob grinning back as if he didn't have a worry in the world. Although it was a national championship, the four best-performed active Australian marathoners, Dave Chettle, Gerard Barrett, Chris Wardlaw and Bill Scott, were all absent for one reason or another and the field was only saved from mediocrity by the presence of four up-and-coming Japanese. It was uneventful until 30 km where Katsuhiro Tashikawa led in 1:36:09 and Rob cruised contentedly in sixth place. This satisfaction was not shared, as Rob soon realized. 'I looked over at the car where Pat and Gayelene were riding and smiled. Gayelene didn't smile back and I could tell from her expression that she wasn't happy with the way things were going. She thought I was being a little bit too light-hearted. I realized I'd better get a move on.'

Gayelene commented, 'He was smiling and winking at me during the whole marathon. I thought he should have been taking a national championship more seriously.'

There were no signs at the refreshment tables to indicate elapsed distance and most of the runners missed the small numbers marked on the surface of the road. Rob's pace had slumped to 16:07 for the 5 km between 25 km and 30 km and Clohessy realized he was losing ground on the leaders. Gayelene's expression told the runner all he needed to know and he accelerated sharply, surging into the lead at 31 km. Only Tashikawa tried to go with him but the sudden kick-down was too much for the Japanese and the young Australian was all alone by 35 km. He completed the course in 2:13:23 to become, at 22, the sixth fastest marathoner in Australian history. Japanese runners took the next four places with Queenslander Robert Stones, the second Australian home, sixth in 2:16:49.

Rob had arrived now as a top Australian marathoner and the power of his finish suggested he had the sort of raw running strength that Derek Clayton considered essential for achieving elite status in the event. The youngster confirmed his metamorphosis to international class four months later when he won the prestigious Emil Zatopek 10,000 m track event on an uncomfortably humid evening in Melbourne. He clocked 28:23.6, inside the Olympic qualifying time and suggesting, as Herne Hill had, that there were better things to come.

As Christmas approached, Rob made a fateful decision to become, for a time, a fulltime runner. On vacation from his course at Swinburne Technical College, he asked Gayelene to join him in Victoria during her university break and they rented a cottage at The Patch in the Dandenongs so they could both spend more time on the roads and bush tracks that had paid so many dividends for other Australian runners. She was recovering from the first of two major surgical repairs to her knees, both of which involved cutting and grafting bone. Such was her determination to run well again that she agreed to a radical rebuilding of one joint that has left her with the appearance of having two kneecaps. But at this stage she was optimistic. She said, 'We had a beautiful time getting to know one another in the isolation of the Dandenongs, doing what we both love most: running. Sometimes, after a morning session, we would have friends around for brunch and we would all just laze about in the sun.'

However, with unlimited time for training, Rob fell into the trap of doing too much. 'I got a bit carried away. My weekly mileage crept up to 245 km (that's 35 km a day, almost all of it on lung-stretching hills) and I started to get minor, nagging injuries. I didn't realize how rundown I was until I went to Melbourne to do a session of track work with Pat. I was running 400s which I usually do in about sixty-three seconds. Pat just kept looking from his stopwatch to me and shaking his head. When he doesn't say anything you know he is really upset. I was clocking 75s and I couldn't go any faster.'

Clohessy was shocked. 'You could see something had gone wrong just by looking at him. He had got himself into a hole and I knew it could take as long as six months to get him out. I told him to take a complete rest even though it meant breaking a training streak of more than 1,000 days. That was a hard thing for him to do but he agreed. He has always been very good about accepting advice.'

The rest seemed to refresh Rob and he was reasonably optimistic about his first big race of the Olympic year, a 10,000 m at the SGIO (State Government Insurance Office) Games in Melbourne featuring triple world record-holder Henry Rono and his compatriot Kiprotich Rono. The event turned into a fascinating duel between Scott and the two Ronos, with the skinny Australian pushing Henry to his second fastest 10,000 m. Rob came in fourth in a PB 28:16.12 and his chances of winning a place in the track team for Moscow looked good. But racing in such a rundown condition took more out of him than he realized. When Scott and Steve Austin began to battle for the lead in the 10,000 m trial race on a windy afternoon in Sydney, Rob found he couldn't respond. He dropped back while tenacious Garry Henry held on for third, leaving Rob fourth — the same as nowhere in an Olympic trial.

All his Moscow eggs were now in the marathon basket. Grimly, he contemplated the trial at West Lakes near Adelaide on Easter Sunday. In this depleted state he would be facing the fastest field of marathoners ever assembled in Australia. His thoughts were far from rosy. 'I was feeling terrible. Every training session was a struggle. Then, strangely, I started to feel normal again just two days before the West Lakes race. I began to think I could be competitive, but I wasn't sure.'

The field included Chettle (2:10:20); Wardlaw (2:11:55); Scott (2:11:55); Barrett (2:12:20); the sharply improving Garry Henry; Rob; and a second division of eight runners whose ambitions were somewhat less than 2:13 and an Olympic singlet. Only Scott was sure of selection in a track event, the 10,000 m, although Barrett had been nominated subject to a fitness test.

At 18 km, Barrett the bespectacled, sun-tanned Queenslander with the satiny stride, surged sharply and opened a break on the five other leaders. By the halfway point he was 200 metres ahead and Rob was trying to ignore some nasty blood blisters and relax in the hard-working pack. Chettle was the first to crack. He dropped his hands to his knees at 25 km, hunched over and watched from the side of the road as seven years of running, planning and hoping receded into the distance.

The four-man pack closed steadily on Barrett until 32 km when he again surged decisively. Three kilometres later Scott, troubled by a foot injury and with his competitive fires dimmed by the security of his 10,000 m selection, followed Chettle to the side of the road.

Barrett now seemed assured of first place and certain selection although he said later, 'I was exhausted by the time we passed 35 km. I just hung on and counted every kilometre.'

There were three runners behind him struggling for the remaining two places in Australia's team: Wardlaw, the little bearded father-figure of the Victorian distance running scene, Rob, his most promising protégé, and Henry, the dogged, pony-tailed physical education student at Pembroke State University in the US. Rob could make little impression on Barrett, but he was too strong for his other rivals in the run for home. Wardlaw battled on with typical grit to get in third, twenty-four seconds ahead of Henry. The times of this fastest all-Australian race were: Barrett, 2:11:42; de Castella, 2:12:24; Wardlaw, 2:12:47; and Henry, 2:13:11. There was a big gap to the other three finishers with Len Johnson clocking 2:22:34, John Stanley 2:27:58 and Ian Doble setting a South Australian veteran's record in seventh place with 2:34:18.

Henry, who had also narrowly missed selection when placed third in the 10,000 m, said, 'I suppose you could say I was unlucky to run 2:13:11 and still finish fourth, but really, the others were better. There is no way I could have run one second faster.'

Henry's time would come.

Despite his first defeat, Rob's marathon graph showed a pleasing upward trend, with his times improving with each race — from 2:14:44 to 2:13:23 to 2:12:24. Remarking later on her son's tolerance of pain, Anne de Castella said, 'He finished the Olympic trials with blood oozing from his shoes. Yet he managed to hobble on to the tennis court that afternoon and partner me in a doubles match.'

Rob observed that it was a good thing his mother was a good player in her own right and didn't have to rely too heavily on his performance.

This fine effort in the trial helped cement his relationship with Clohessy. Rob commented, 'Pat knew how much trouble I was in before the race and I think the fact that I performed so well impressed him more than anything else I had done. Especially when he realized later that things were still not quite right with me, even after the race.'

In retrospect, Clohessy regarded the trial as an unfortunate episode as far as Australia's overall distance running strength was concerned. Within a few years Barrett, Wardlaw and Henry had all undergone serious surgery which dislocated their careers, Scott had been forced into premature retirement by his foot problem and Chettle's star had waned. Clohessy summed up the event, saying 'It was a terribly hard race with five good runners fighting desperately for three Games places. I'm afraid several of them damaged themselves. It would have been better if Scott and Barrett had bypassed the race and relied on their selections for track events.'

But selectors and budgets had previously robbed Barrett of a Games place when he was running well before the 1978 Commonwealth meeting in Edmonton. Who could blame him, or Scott, for seeking the extra security of a multiple qualification?

After the trial Rob flew to Perth to join Gayelene in a flat close to the university and to King's Park where they trained every day.

CHAPTER EIGHT

Misha and all that

During the week after the Australian Olympic trial, Rob officially achieved a ten year-old ambition when his name was added to the list of Australian competitors for the Moscow Games. The Amateur Athletic Union of Australia (AAU) announced that the three trial place-getters, Barrett, de Castella and Wardlaw, along with Clohessy and road walker Tim Erickson, would be added to the track and field squad already nominated for the Games. The party of thirty-one competitors, three coaches and two managers faced one last bureaucratic hurdle before settling into final preparations: approval by the justifications committee of the Australian Olympic Federation (AOF) which had the power to cull the AAU nominations.

Clohessy, as usual, was optimistic. 'I have a lot of confidence in our distance running contingent for Moscow. I have great respect for the ability of people like Steve Austin and Bill Scott, even though I don't coach them. Austin is a very real chance in Moscow.'

When the AOF approved his nomination that Friday, Rob was left with two remaining problems. The first was physical: the West Lakes run had taken more out of him than either of his two previous marathons and as he plunged back into his training routines he waited anxiously for some sign that his former zest was returning. The second problem was political, and essentially beyond his control. Like many other marathoners he had started 1980 with more interest in his training log than in newspaper headlines. You have to be

Trying to break away from Rod Dixon in a road race in New Zealand. The versatile Kiwi joined the sub-2:09 marathon club when he won the New York race in late 1983.

Life is not just running. Rob and Gayelene glow with the pride of a different sort of achievement after his graduation as a Bachelor of Applied Science. The ceremony, at which Deek gave the oration, was delayed until 1983 by his overseas racing engagements.

single-minded to seriously tackle an Olympic marathon. Few runners in the advanced stages of their Olympic preparations took time to ponder all the possibilities arising from the Soviet invasion of Afghanistan in late 1979. When the US President, Jimmy Carter, swung his sporting counter-punch to Brezhnev's tanks, gunships and bombs, it landed on a lot of unguarded athletic chins. Boycott the Games? It was unthinkable.

Alan Attwood of the *Age* rang Rob for comment and then wrote: 'Robert de Castella lives to run: twice a day, seven days a week. Suddenly he is not sure where he is running to. Until a few days ago, he thought the 240 km of roads and forest tracks he runs along each week all led to Moscow. Now he does not know where they go, or even what all the running was for.'

These were early days in the Carter campaign. The politically beleagured President, thrashing around for a response to Brezhnev's brazen aggression and needing to camouflage his inability to take any real geo-political action, had not yet been able to coerce the US Olympic Committee to a politician's point of view. Rob was still hopeful and told Attwood: 'The Games are a long way off yet. I wouldn't want to get too emotionally carried away...but the possibility, the thought that they could be called off is pretty terrifying. The issue for the Prime Minister [Malcolm Fraser] is political. We're not politicians, we're athletes. You can't dissociate athletes from the Olympics — they are an athletic issue. A boycott is a short-term thing. How many people remember that the Africans boycotted the Montreal Games? The only people who really suffered were the athletes concerned. The Olympics are not just another venue. The Games are the best athletes competing in an incredible atmosphere against each other...something worth sacrificing about everything to participate in.'

Carter's early campaign flushed a fairly enthusiastic response from what the Americans like to call 'friendly nations'. Right-wing dictators in Paraguay and Chile rushed to sign up, and conservative Western governments showed interest, although it soon became obvious they would have trouble coercing their national Olympic committees, a problem that didn't worry the South Americans. There was an embarrassing moment when Carter's White House staff showed how little they knew of the sports -politics situation by sending a message inviting South Africa to join the crusade. It was just twenty years since a Springbok athlete had been admitted to an Olympic meeting. One can imagine the thigh-slapping laughter and Afrikaans wisecracks that followed the reception of that telex in Pretoria.

The South Africans had been expelled from international competition for bringing politics (that is, the apartheid philosophy) into the way they administered sports and selected their national teams. The initial boycotts — which contributed a great deal towards improving the lot of non-white sportsmen in South Africa — were a sporting response to a sporting problem. It could be argued, particularly in track and field, that the sporting problem had now been substantially corrected and that the continuing ostracism of the republic's sportsmen of all races had degenerated into a sporting response to a political problem. Of course, much is blurred along the boundaries of sporting and political life. But if sporting solutions were sought for all the world's non-sporting, political problems, international sport would soon cease to exist.

Unlike those imposed on South Africa, Carter's boycott started out blatantly and unashamedly as a sporting response to a political problem. Carter needed a high-profile response to Soviet aggression, but his electorate was in no mood for creeping military involvement in the Vietnam style. He was also handicapped by sensible fears of a nuclear war and by the fact that the Soviet Union was stronger than the US in its ability to wage conventional warfare. A trade boycott would devastate American grain producers and a strategic materials boycott was not enough in itself. But to sit around doing nothing would be to court defeat in the next presidential election.

The idea of an Olympic boycott promised political deliverance. It would require little sacrifice from anybody except the athletes (a tiny number in electoral terms) would need little administrative effort but would garner intense publicity. All that had to be established to permit a presidential decree forbidding participation was the fact that the Afghanistan invasion was a threat to the security of the US. That was as easy as a telephone call to the Pentagon.

The telex to South Africa demonstrated how little Carter's politicians knew of the world of sportsmen. What did it matter to Washington power-brokers that the Olympics, although often abused, were founded and existed in a spirit of international fraternity and were held every four years on temporarily neutral territory handed over by a sovereign State, the host nation, to the Olympic administrators for the duration of competition? The 1980 Olympics were not Russia's Games, no matter how hard the Russians would try to wring propaganda value from them. But the concept of the Games as an institution shared by the sportswomen and sportsmen of all nations, rather than owned by the host nation, was a subtle one to try to sell to people whose business was to push the opposite view.

Carter's call was well received in Australia. Fraser had his own political problems and had worked hard throughout his years as prime minister to strengthen the US–Australian alliance. A popular campaign against such a repugnant act as the Afghanistan adventure would do no harm to his image. He had been a constant critic of the Russians and, like Carter, wished to appear more than passive about their aggression. His National Country Party allies would not have countenanced a total trade embargo and the loss of wheat and wool exports to the Soviet Union. His response would have to be something less, but something that attracted a good deal of publicity. The Olympic boycott came as a godsend.

The press, particularly the Murdoch and Fairfax chains, rallied forcefully behind the idea. Rupert Murdoch had a luncheon meeting with Carter in the US and although the topic was finance, the conversation, apparently, passed to other matters. Afterwards Murdoch rang Les Hollings, editor of his flagship, the *Australian*, in Sydney, and the next issue of the national daily carried a front page editorial pushing a boycott and also splashed the latest developments. The first thunderous shots had been fired in the country's fiercest press campaign since the sacking of the Whitlam Labor Government in 1975.

The word *traitors* was used more than once as Australia's sportsmen stood up to the politicians and said they wanted to go to Moscow, regardless of the weight of argument ranged against them. The AOF met on the issue and decided Australia should only join a boycott that was shown to be effective and truly international. Wardlaw, a natural tilter at windmills, formed an athletes' lobby group in a brave attempt to counter the vast media and political armoury assembled to bring about a boycott. He became embroiled in the newspaper and television debates, putting across the pro-Olympic viewpoint in an articulate and sometimes impassioned way and took more than his share of criticism as a result. Among the flak he received from the fringes of public life were several death threats. The struggle was so intense it undermined his chances of competing at his best in Moscow.

There were proposals for an alternative Free Games to rival the Olympics, including an American suggestion that they should be staged in Melbourne. After a meeting of top athletes, Wardlaw announced, 'We cannot be a party to an alternative games as is being proposed by the proponents of an Olympic boycott. To be a party to such a substitute event would only contribute to the destruction of the Olympic movement.'

Wardlaw believed the athletes saw the Olympic Games as a means of bringing people closer together, not pushing them apart. The Olympics were a world and international event and did not belong to any bloc. Sporting competition had helped ease Cold War tensions in the past, he said. The International Olympic Federation eventually vetoed the Free Games idea.

On 14 April, little more than a week after Rob's selection was confirmed, Australians learned that the US Olympic Committee had voted, after being addressed by the nation's Vice-president Walter Mondale, to obey the call for a boycott. The meeting's resolution read, in part: 'Since the President advised the committee that in the light of international events the security of the country is threatened, the committee has decided not to send a team.'

Fraser responded, 'I believe now an effective boycott will emerge.'

But the president of the AOF, Syd Grange, said Australian participation would still depend on the development of a truly international boycott. The key issue became the question of participation by the major nations of western Europe.

Meanwhile, Wardlaw rejected claims that the struggle had already undermined the motivation and morale of Australia's athletes. In a letter to the *Australian* he said: 'The Olympics are important to an athlete who has devoted many hours (to training), by choice. But their existence is not in any sense a sole motivating factor towards the pursuit of excellence in any sporting endeavour. I have trained this morning and will train again this afternoon, regardless of pronouncements by politicians about possible boycotts and by Olympic officials about possible uncertainty and its effects on athletes in training. I participated in Montreal in 1976 and have aimed for the past four years to be at Moscow. I do not believe sport is above politics. Nor is education, the arts, nor indeed is anything which involves individuals and their inter-relations with society. Sport and the Olympics can be considered a tool towards harmony and peace, but never considered above oppression and imperialism.'

He argued that the Olympics, although they could not be extricated from politics, should not become simply an arm of any nation's foreign policy.

At the height of the debate, figures released in Canberra showed that Australia had just achieved record wheat and wool sales to the Soviet Union. Questioned on the matter, the Deputy Prime Minister, Doug Anthony, said the Government had no need to apologize. 'This is normal trade. We have entered into substantial contracts with the Soviet Union prior to their invasion of Afghanistan. Those contracts are now being honoured.'

In one of many published interviews, Wardlaw mused on the problems of his counter-campaign. 'It's difficult to fight people like Malcolm Fraser who spent $2,000 last week on telegrams over the issue. I spent $9 on my telegram stating my case. How can I compete? It's going to be an uphill battle but I am prepared to fight to the bitter end. We are prepared to fight until we go down screaming.'

He said the athletes could go to Moscow as individuals, paying their own way. But this would cost them at least $5,000 each. As his anger rose at the thought of what the politicians were doing to the sportsmen, he told the interviewer: 'Malcolm Fraser is not an Olympian, never has been and never could be. It is not his right to impose a boycott on us.'

Wardlaw, Rob and the others pressed on with their training as best they could while the battle raged around them.

When the International Olympic Federation voted to proceed with the Moscow Games, the rift between politician and sportsman grew even wider. Fraser was still determined Australia would boycott the meeting and stressed that a $500,000 government grant to the AOF should not be used to transport athletes to Moscow. A number of major sponsors also withdrew support and the AOF's general-secretary, Judy Patching, commented, 'The funding programme has been hurt a great deal. We have a lot of ground to make up. We're in a precarious position.'

Following talks between the Government and the AOF, Fraser

released to the press a copy of a letter he had given to the sporting officials. It read: 'Before you come to your final view, I would like you to ask yourselves what, in your view, would be sufficient cause for the Games to be moved or have Australians not attend. Is it that an invasion of Afghanistan is not a sufficient invasion? Have the Soviets not used enough troops to give sufficient cause? Or is the population of Afghanistan too small for it to matter enough? How many Soviet troops would need to be used in that invasion, occupation and suppression before Moscow, in your view, would become an inappropriate site? If the invasion were of a country closer to Australia, or closer to Europe, would that alter your judgement? I ask these questions because I am sure you will agree with me at some point, an invasion, occupation and suppression of a people would be sufficient cause for an abandonment of the Games.'

Nobody in the media raised a voice against this blatant attempt by a politician, ultimately in charge of foreign policy, to shift his responsibility on to a committee whose sole purpose was the administration of sport. It would certainly have been politically safer to browbeat the sportsmen into making the decision and accepting the blame than to risk acting in an authoritarian manner, say by refusing to issue passports to the team members. There was always the danger of a civil rights backlash.

On 19 April, 103 training days before the marathon was due to be run in Moscow, the AOF met in Melbourne and announced it would be sending its team to the Olympic Games. The same week, the *Sydney Morning Herald* carried a photo of Wardlaw and Scott, in their green-and-gold striped Olympic blazers, leaving for Europe en route to Moscow. A headline beside the picture and attached to a separate but associated story said: 'They'll run for roubles...'

With the AOF decision, the boycott battle was all over bar the shouting, although there was still plenty of that from both sides of Parliament, on TV and, figuratively, in the columns of the newspapers. The Australian situation was mirrored in other Western democracies where governments backed the boycott but national Olympic committees took a contrary view and eventually prevailed. There was particular bitterness in Britain where the Prime Minister, Margaret Thatcher, campaigned strenuously for a boycott only to be defied by the sportsmen. Within weeks she would be doing her best to exploit a wave of patriotic enthusiasm stirred by British gold medal exploits in Lenin Stadium.

The final comment on the whole exercise came on 10 July 1981, when a fullscale, official US track and field team competed against the USSR in Leningrad. Nothing had changed in Afghanistan.

While Wardlaw and Scott were in Europe preparing for the Games, Rob continued to train from his temporary home in Perth while he waited to leave with the main Games party. Clohessy, who was keeping a close, concerned watch on his progress, said, 'He wasn't quite out of the hole he had got himself into with over-training. We just had to hope he would come right in time.'

Preparing mentally for a race in which a substantial and very forceful group of your countrymen said you should not compete, was not an easy matter. The runners were frequently criticised in letters to newspapers, with the words *callous*, *indifferent*, *selfish* and *disloyal* appearing regularly. But, perhaps because he was in Perth, Rob did not suffer personally in the way Wardlaw did. One evening when he was showering after training Gayelene answered a knock on the door to find a young man who asked, 'Is this where Rob de Castella lives?'

She countered with a cautious 'Why?'

The young man said, 'I want to congratulate him on having the courage to go to the Olympics.'

When he was invited inside, he shook Rob's hand and said, 'My university friends and I just wanted to let you know that we are proud to be living in the same block of flats as an Australian Olympian.'

Rob's Olympic build-up was punctuated by only one personal piece of unpleasantness. The Melbourne radio announcer, Derryn Hinch, who is noted for his adherence to fashionable causes, took the Olympic athletes to task over the air and named Rob, along with Wardlaw. Three years later when Hinch wanted Rob to speak on air after one of his successes in the US, the runner declined until Hinch made the reasons for Rob's reluctance clear to his listeners.

Unfortunately, the whole Olympic experience in 1980 was a world removed from the participation in a mission of national glory that Games competition had been in simpler days. But at least the Australians retained their right to attend. The Americans had held full Olympic trials in spite of the boycott moves and the women and men who won through had then to suffer the bitter frustration of the USOC decision. Japan followed America's lead, depriving her splendid marathoners, Toshihiko Seko, Takeshi Soh and Shigeru Soh, of the chance of glory. Kenya also stayed at home, so runners such as Mike Boit, the Commonwealth 800 m champion, lost their chance to atone for missing the 1976 Olympics because of another boycott. That one was orchestrated by the Supreme Council for Sport in Africa because New Zealand was attending and had rugby union ties with South Africa. By the time of the Los Angeles Olympics, Kenya's marvellous runners would have been out of Olympic competition for twelve years — several lifetimes in athletic terms.

The Japanese, and to a lesser extent the Americans, would be the major absentees from the marathon. The defending champion, Waldemar Cierpinski of East Germany, would be there, along with a strong trio of Soviet runners. The British looked impressive with Ian Thompson, Bernie Ford and Dave Black, and the year's fastest man, Gerard Nijboer of the Netherlands, was a certain starter. Africa's best active marathoner, Kebede Balcha of Ethiopia, would be pursuing the great traditions of his nation and, most intriguing, the immortal Finnish track runner Lasse Viren, gold medallist in both the 5,000 m and 10,000 m in 1972 and 1976, was said to be mainly interested in the marathon this time. He had placed fifth in the long run when he contested it, apparently as an afterthought, at the Montreal Games.

There was plenty to think about as Rob and the other distance runners from Australia explored the training venues and streets and boulevardes of Moscow, the often grim, mysterious capital of the Russians' vast Euro-Asian empire. Reports despatched to Australia commented on an odd absence of children in the streets and parks and claimed they had been moved out of town to avoid being polluted by contact with 'corrupt Westerners'. Rob and the other distance runners began their training runs around the streets until some Russian athletes in a van stopped beside them one day and managed to communicate the fact that there was a forest nearby that was much better for training than the streets. They gave the Australians a lift to the area and they trained there every day after that, remarking wryly to each other about the number of children playing in the woods and nearby parks. 'They must be cardboard cutouts,' said Wardlaw.

'But what about their voices?' Rob asked.

'Oh that's an old commie trick. They can do anything with tapes, you know.'

The long Olympic track races, as usual, brought shock failures and upsets, with the wizened Ethiopian Miruts Yifter triumphant in both the 5,000 m and 10,000 m. In the longer run, Scott made the final and finished ninth in 28:15.1. It was well outside his personal best but conditions were far from ideal and he finished ahead of the redoubtable Englishmen Brendan Foster and Mike McLeod among others.

The Australian 5,000 m men scraped through to the semi-finals but were then eliminated — Dave Fitzsimons in 10th place in 13:58.3 and Austin 11th in 13:47.6. Fitzsimons was 0.1 second behind the future world record-holder Dave Moorcroft in his semi while Austin finished less than a second behind Alex Hagelsteens who was soon to become one of the fastest 10,000 m men in history. The logic of distance running fortunes can be vague.

The Australian marathon men pondered the lessons of the long track runs and inspected the course they would soon be racing over. It was flat and seemed as if it would be fast, with sheltering trees along a good deal of its length. Hot weather had devastated the track events and would obviously be a problem. The Aussies agreed that a time of 2:10 would certainly win the race and that Viren, 31, was the one to beat. Wardlaw's opinion was definite. 'I think Viren has been set up for this marathon all along and that is how he seemed to run the 10,000 m. That he was still up there at the bell proves he has more pace than any other marathon exponent at present. He still runs strongly and he is the man to beat.'

Accustomed by now to being a spokesman to the media, Wardlaw told Australian pressmen that Cierpinski and Russia's European champion, Leonid Moseyev, would be strong performers. He added that the three Australians were among those with chances and, given the breaks, any of them could run out the winner.

But it turned out to be a strange and disappointing race. Rob's one-word summary was 'crazy'.

Despite the boycott, thirteen of the year's twenty fastest marathoners started and the quality and experience of the field should have guaranteed some commonsense in the way the race was run. But a combination of high ambition and fear of the 26 degree weather led to a pace that fluctuated so wildly only fifty-three of the seventy-three starters were able to complete the course. The 5 km splits were above fifteen minutes between 10 km and 20 km, then the tempo increased suddenly to 14:13, slowed progressively through 15:33 to 16:20 before accelerating again to 14:47 between 35 km and

40 km. Barrett was one of the twenty casualties when he finally conceded, after 25 km, that achilles tendon and back problems would not allow him to do himself justice.

Vladimir Kotov, who had won the Soviet championship earlier in the year, led the way from the stadium at a comparative dawdle and when an obscure Dane, Jorn Lauenborg, tried to pick up the pace nobody was willing to go with him. Lauenborg ran through 5 km in 15:48 while Rob and Wardlaw followed in a cautious main group twenty-two seconds back. Kotov went after the Dane in the next 5 km and led the way past 10 km in 31:16 with a pack (horde?) of about forty stalking him from twenty seconds back. Rob was running comfortably at the back of the group but Wardlaw was in trouble. He had had diarrhoea the previous day but had put that down to nerves. Now he found he couldn't even keep water down. At 18 km he started to buckle over with stomach cramps and he had to fight to stay with the pace. He said later, 'I had had a lot of hassles, although that's not a real excuse. You have to do what you can regardless of the circumstances. After campaigning against the boycott I got to a flat in London and just collapsed there for three weeks. I just switched off and watched television the whole time. The arguments were still raging in my mind. I was sending letters back and going over points and counter-points. I was being attacked back in Australia. A runner's responsible for his own psychological preparation, but this was a very special circumstance. It made the race the toughest I have ever run.'

Kotov led through 20 km in 1:03:42 but he now had the close company of about twenty-five runners, including Cierpinski, Viren and the Britons Black and Ford. Thompson, who suffered stomach trouble, had dropped out.

Enter ambition, in the form of the balding Mexican Rodolfo Gomez. He strode past Kotov on the flat, tree-shaded boulevarde along the river and clapped on the pace. He bolted through 5 km in 14:13, leaving ruin in his wake. Viren, whose pale skin was glowing pink in the strong sunshine, dropped out at 27 km, followed by Black, who had rubbed a toe raw and Ford who just went to pieces (the quality English newspapers misinterpreted runners' jargon and described him reeling from the road and colliding with a wall, instead of merely Hitting The Wall). Wardlaw started to lose his rhythm. He felt vague and although he was aware he was running erratically he

74

could do nothing to correct himself. Rob had his usual blisters and felt a couple of toenails lifting, but despite these discomforts he was still in the competition. Cierpinski exercised the prudence of experience and dropped 48 seconds behind the charging Mexican.

Nijboer, the tall, muscular Dutchman who had run 2:09:01 earlier in the year, Kotov and his two teammates Moseyev and Satymkul Dzhumanazarov, were closest to Gomez as he continued to lead through 30 km and 35 km. A long way behind the leaders, Wardlaw vomited and was able to settle into something like a rhythm afterwards. He didn't know whether he could finish and remembered ten runners passing him between the 35 km and 40 km refreshments tables. But he kept going.

At about 32 km Rob began to struggle and became aware that he could no longer hope to make any headway on the leaders.

Meanwhile, Cierpinski's sensible, even pacing over the previous 15 km had brought him back into contact with the boom-and-bust Mexican. At 35 km the defending champion was running beside Nijboer and only three seconds behind Gomez. Six or seven other runners, including the three Russians, were still in touch. Ron Clarke, doing the commentary for Australian TV, said, 'Cierpinski's looking good! He's looking cool and has good rhythm.'

The East German later commented, 'It was hard to choose the right moment to increase the pace ... that was the most critical decision of the race ... it was a very hard run.'

It was a measure of his ability that he was more concerned about timing than execution. Execution was all that mattered now to the Australians. Rob was concentrating to hold his form to the finish and Wardlaw was struggling to put one foot after the other.

At 35 km Nijboer lifted his pace and passed Gomez. Cierpinski, who was shadowing the Dutchman, said later, 'It was at the thirty-fifth kilometre that I began to feel a little bit sure of victory.'

The East German, running with his characteristic high arm action and smooth rhythm, seemed to surge effortlessly at 36 km and was nineteen seconds clear by 40 km which he passed in 2:04:35. But it wasn't as easy as it seemed. Looking back on the event, he remarked, 'With two kilometres to go I was almost certain of victory but, curiously, I had some fear at that moment because the last two kilometres were particularly painful.'

Despite the hurt, the chalky-skinned Olympic champion was able to sprint the final 200 m in 33.4 to win in 2:11:03. Nijboer finished without a matching flourish to take the silver medal in 2:11:20 while the little Central Asian, Dzhumanazarov, pulled away from Kotov and Moseyev to take the bronze medal in 2:11:35. Gomez came in fifth behind the three Soviet runners and ahead of Dereje Nedi (Ethiopia), Massimo Magnani (Italy) and the seasoned and consistent Karel Lismont (Belgium).

Rob was tenth in 2:14:31, the fastest time run by an Australian in an Olympic race and the highest placing after Derek Clayton's seventh in 1968 and Ron Clarke's ninth in 1964. Gayelene, waiting at home to see him enter the stadium, was frustrated like so many other Australians when the TV coverage cut off at the precise moment of his entry. It was the first time Rob had failed to score a PB in a marathon. Yet he was philosophical about the run. 'I was satisfied with the effort. My training hadn't been that good and the uncertainty and conflict caused by the boycott made it difficult to build up mentally for the race.'

Clohessy was, as usual, encouraging. 'To run that fast in such a difficult race after having a lot of trouble recovering from over-training was a tribute to Deek. It was faster than Clayton or Clarke ever achieved in the Olympics.'

Wardlaw's brave fight ended after two hours, twenty minutes and forty-two seconds. He finished in twenty-eighth place and had to put up with the final indignity of being the crowd's villain in a last-lap struggle with the tiny North Korean, Chun Son Goe. The 30-year-old Australian faced a long, difficult struggle to recapture his competitive zest. 'It was the worst I have ever felt after a marathon,' he said. 'I just folded up in the changing rooms. When the others left to board the minibus I tried to follow them and I just couldn't stand up. I nearly fainted. I had to slump back on a bench and I was calling desperately: "Pat, Pat..."'

'Then, when they got me on the bus, I was in agony with cramp. The sensible thing when you are running that badly is to pull out, but when it's the Olympics and you have waited four years and fought a political campaign for the chance to compete in them...'

In his next marathon, in Peking in 1982, Wardlaw could manage a time of only 2:38.

Clohessy and Rob noted the timing of Cierpinski's decisive move — in the final 10 km — and the way he orchestrated his own pacing to ignore the madness at the front of the field. They were important lessons to be absorbed. They were aware the young Australian would soon do better than an honourable tenth in 2:14:31 and when an invitation arrived for the Fukuoka Marathon in Japan which was run every year on the first Sunday in December, they began planning a major effort.

CHAPTER NINE

In Camelot

The busy port of Fukuoka nestles in a coastal indentation in the north-west corner of the southern Japanese island of Kyushu. It was little more than a fishing village until Japan shrugged off its cloak of isolation last century; then it grew quickly because of its strategic location in relation to the Asian mainland. Like all modern ports it attracted industry, but not on the crushing, pollution-spewing scale of Yokohama or Osaka. It became Westernized, but not to the same degree as Tokyo. In the 1980s much of the residential housing was still in the wood-and-ricepaper tradition and the old style of dress had not become unusual enough to be a curiosity.

But Fukuoka had come to be more than a place name. Like Wimbledon, it conjures visions of sporting excellence. Like the English village with its unofficial world tennis championship, Fukuoka had become an annual meeting place for a sport's elite. Each year since 1965 the cream of the world's marathoners had gathered there to joust with each other over a horseshoe out-and-back course from Heiwadei Stadium in the city's centre, through the industrial zone and residential suburbs, to a coastal resort and back again. The road surface is not particularly good although the course is fast, with only one minor hill at the 41 km mark. Some of the fastest runs in history have unfolded there and results over the years are crowded with PBs.

The secret of all this success is the way the race is organized and the atmosphere it engenders. The committee always extends all-

78

expenses invitations to six world-class runners who are judged on performances in the preceding twelve months. Since the race is at the end of the year, the organizers can review a full year's competition and it offers ambitious runners the chance to score vital points at year's end to improve their world ranking — and their subsequent invitations to other marathons. Any sub-2:20 marathoner who wants to run and gets himself to Japan will have all his expenses covered by the committee while he is in the country and any runner who has beaten 2:27 in the previous twelve months may enter at his own expense.

This last category caters mainly for up-and-coming Japanese who have a splendid tradition to follow in the event, the rigours of which seem to mesh well with the national virtues of discipline, diligence and self-sacrificing courage. Japan's only gold medal for an Olympic running event was won by Kitei Son at Hitler's Games in 1936 when another Japanese, Shoryu Nan, was third. It was incidental at the time that Son was a Korean; he was a citizen of the Japanese Empire. Soon after that success, sport was pushed to the fringes of the nation's life by the upheavals of war, the Occupation and intense Western-style industrialization. As a middle class emerged in the 1950s and leisure began to play a more important role in life, Japan produced a long line of excellent marathon performers. Takayuki Nakao was the fastest in the world in 1961 with 2:18:54, Kokichi Tsuburaya took the bronze medal in the 1964 Olympics and Morio Shigematsu shattered Abebe Bikila's world record when he ran 2:12:00 in 1965. That year Japanese runners amassed an unprecedented total of forty points in the US magazine *Track and Field News'* annual rankings. It was also the year of the first Fukuoka Invitation Marathon.

The inaugural event was won by New Zealander Mike Ryan and the race has been a productive one for Aussies and Kiwis ever since. Derek Clayton broke his first world record there when he ran 2:09:36 in the third edition of the event in 1967 and that mark was to remain the race record for fourteen years, despite the best efforts of the world's finest marathoners. The impact of the event on Australian fortunes is graphically illustrated by this 1984 best-ever list:

1	Rob de Castella	2:08:18	Fukuoka	1981
2	Derek Clayton	2:08:34	Antwerp	1969
3	Garry Henry	2:10:09	Fukuoka	1980

4	Dave Chettle	2:10:20	Fukuoka	1975
5	John Farrington	2:11:13	Richmond	1973
6	Gerard Barrett	2:11:42	West Lakes	1980
7	Chris Wardlaw	2:11:55	Fukuoka	1979
8	Bill Scott	2:11:55	Fukuoka	1979

The race is sponsored by the *Asahi Shimbun* newspaper and the runners are treated like VIPs from the moment they arrive, with civic receptions, press conferences, dinners and pre-race workouts all closely monitored by the media. The two hours and fifteen minutes of the quality end of the race are televised live throughout Japan and such shoe companies as Nike, Tiger and New Balance pursue this valuable exposure by paying runners' expenses to represent them at the race. Events like the Nike Gathering of Eagles in Eugene, Oregon, offer trips to Fukuoka as winners' prizes.

One of the Australians to score a PB there, Len Johnson, who writes as well as he can run, had this to say about the atmosphere before the 1978 race when he clocked 2:19:32: 'The training course consists of a path around the local lake. I don't know what the course record is but no matter how fast you run you are continually buzzed by local runners who seem permanently stuck in top gear. They must be the descendants of the kamikaze runners Rob McKinney (the first sub-2:20 Australian) had warned me about, the ones who try to reach the turn in an hour. The build-up continues with trips to have a look at the course and run part of it, photographers everywhere we trained and people pointing us out everywhere we went in town. By this time I was getting so high, training runs were turning into PBs over 16 km.'

The early winter weather is almost always kind and the course is lined with excited, knowledgeable people waving little paper Japanese flags and those of other competing nations. (Who was it who likened the noise to 'the rustling of monstrous cicada wings'?) The crowd support is a great help to the competitors, especially the Japanese who ended seven years of North American monopoly on first placing when they went 1–2–3 in 1978 and then repeated the feat in 1979.

For the 1980 race, Rob had the company of the new Australian champion, Lawrie Whitty, 21, and of Garry Henry, 25, the hard-luck runner of the Australian Olympic trials earlier in the year when he had just missed out over both 10,000 m and the marathon. Henry had

The moment that thrilled a nation: Rob forges past Juma Ikangaa for a third and final time to take control of the Brisbane Commonwealth Games marathon after being in an apparently hopeless situation at the halfway mark.

The tension, the pain and the uncertainty evaporate as Rob gallops to the finish to become Commonwealth Marathon Champion.

since won the Vancouver Marathon, placed second in the Montreal Marathon in a PB of 2:11:37 and logged an average of 175 km/week as he prepared for a big effort in the Camelot of the long event.

The field was as strong as any since 1965 and was particularly interesting as it brought together the runners who excelled in Moscow and those from the boycotting nations. The four best Olympic performers, Cierpinski, Nijboer, Dzhumanarazov and Kotov, all arrived to put their reputations on the line against Japan's big four, Toshihiko Seko, Takeshi Soh, Sigeru Soh and Kunimitsu Itoh, and the leading Americans Bill Rodgers, Craig Virgin and John Lodwick. There was a world championship atmosphere and there was talk around the hotels and training tracks of a new world record.

The skies were clear, but it was cool and there was a breeze favouring the runners on the outward leg as the gun fired at noon. With so many stars in the field, tactics were on everybody's mind and the pace was left to one of the lesser-known foreigners, Bill Britten from Canada. He was a 2:20 runner and not suicidal and Seko observed later that he realized the chance of a world record had slipped when they went through the first 5 km in the low 15:20s. Still nobody wanted to relieve Britten of his burden and an elite pack of ten runners trailed him through 10 km (31:05), 15 km (46:48) and 20 km (1:02:41). Rob and Garry Henry were running comfortably in the company of the four leading Japanese, the American Kirk Pfeffer and the Englishman Dave Cannon. Cierpinski was looming about ten metres back but Whitty had dropped more than a minute off the pace.

The halfway time was a comparatively modest 1:06:13 but when Rob ran into the lead just after the turnabout the tempo increased noticeably. However, he had not yet reached the stage of development where he could set out to dominate, rather than just survive, an elite marathon. He explained: 'I had no preconceived tactics. Marathon races, at this stage, generally evolved according to the way you felt. I didn't go to the lead with the intention of burning anybody off. I just felt really relaxed and comfortable and found myself there.'

Seko perceived the Australian's move differently. 'From the 25 km to the 30 km was a little fast and I thought, "Only a few of us will still be able to go to the end."'

Henry moved up to run with his countryman and they brought the splits down from 15:53 (15 km–20 km) to 15:14 (20–25) and then 15:07 (25–30) with Rob leading through 30 km in 1:33:02.

That was enough to make the leaders feel the strain but it still wasn't quick enough for Itoh, a tiny man with superb rhythm and a permanent expression of frozen surprise. He whipped to the front and chopped the 5 km pace down to 14:45. Pfeffer's comment was, 'Once that Japanese took off, I just held on by the skin of my teeth.'

Henry, the man with the bushranger looks and the doggedness of Ned Kelly, also hung on, but the gods who rule over the marathon apparently were not convinced Rob had yet paid all his dues. Just when things were poised for a really spectacular performance (his blisters were hurting, but not too much), he was doubled over by a searing stomach cramp. His splits from 25–40 km showed he slowed from 15:07 to 15:20 to 15:31, hardly a disastrous collapse but enough to stop his challenge for a top placing and a sub-2:10. 'The pain was very sharp and I just couldn't accelerate when the Japanese clapped on the pace,' he said.

Gayelene, watching the national TV coverage at the stadium, saw the gods strike. 'Everything seemed to be going well when he suddenly buckled over and grabbed his side. The cameras stayed with the leaders and he just disappeared from sight. I thought he must have dropped out. Then, a few minutes later, a little head appeared in the background. It had a big, un-Japanese moustache and I knew he was back.'

Seko, who had won the previous year in a three-way sprint finish with the Soh-and-Sohs, said, 'Itoh and Takeshi Soh were very good and I followed them. The race followed the same pattern as last year with the final 200 m to the finish line being the real race.'

As Seko followed and then outsprinted his countrymen, Henry followed Seko and was almost close enough to pick up Itoh and snatch third place. He finished fourth in 2:10:09 to become Australia's fastest marathoner since Derek Clayton and one of only two Australians to beat Rob in the long run. Behind Henry, Shigeru Soh finished well to overhaul Cierpinski inside the stadium and take fifth place. The skin of Pfeffer's teeth was enough to get him across the line ahead of Rob who finished eighth in a PB 2:10:44. The race was so close the top eight runners were all on the 400 m track at the same time. It was an event of remarkable depth with two runners under 2:10 for the first time in history and eight under 2:11. Seven of the first nine finishers scored PBs and the times for places two to twenty-two were all the fastest in history for those placings. Seko, who won his third successive Fukuoka, clocked a PB 2:09:45 and Takeshi Soh came home in 2:09:49. Whitty was twentieth in 2:15:33.

Seko told the after-race press conference: 'I didn't expect to break 2:10 because the early pace was so slow. Considering the slow pace, I think the time is a good one.'

Seko's performance made a lasting impression on Rob, who said, 'He is very strong mentally and his running is so controlled. I began to think he would be the hardest marathoner in the world to beat. He holds himself back until the finish and has the strength to back up his speed, which has given him very good times on the track.'

Meanwhile, it was Garry Henry's day and the man who began marathon racing when he was thirteen (3:10:36) and sometimes ran the equivalent of two marathons in a single day's training was deservedly in the Australian limelight. Henry's coach Martin Thompson expressed confidence that his runner would soon go under 2:10, but the new US collegiate record-holder disagreed. 'There is no way I could have gone any faster,' he said. 'The nine seconds doesn't seem much but believe me it is. Perhaps you just need to do more training.'

Henry's effort came as a bolt from the blue to outsiders, but the Australian runners who knew him and had struggled with him for Olympic team places earlier in the year were not so surprised. Gerard Barrett commented, 'Henry ran a bit faster than I thought he would, but it was hard to say what he would do. He's a real trier. Perhaps not the sort to win a big race like Fukuoka but he would stay up there with the leaders for a very long time. He's a very hard man to drop.'

Unfortunately for Henry and Australia, his heavy marathon programme in 1980 took its toll and an achilles tendon injury slowed him down in following years. Clohessy believed that he simply accepted too many marathon invitations.

Barrett retained his faith in Rob. 'Deek's good time didn't surprise me. It was about what I expected of him. In fact, I wouldn't have been surprised if he had gone as fast as Henry.'

The quote of the race came from Seko's coach Kiyoshi Nakamura, who modestly admits to being a messenger of God. On Seko's failure (in the eyes of some Japanese journalists) to achieve a world record, Nakamura said, 'To win in the big race is one thing, and to have a fast time is quite another. It is so difficult to win with best time: like wife and mistress of her husband shake hands.'

Rob faced one extra discomfort after the finish. 'I noticed these guys in white coats bustling about among the runners, looking at their feet. When they got to me they used sign language to get me to pull my shoes off and then became really excited when they saw blood on my socks. They had instruments like big hypodermics and insisted on washing out each blister in turn. It was agonizing and I made a mental note to make sure I had a pair of clean, unbloodied socks available at the finish the next time I ran in Fukuoka.'

After the race Gayelene and Rob went off on a belated honeymoon, travelling by train to the small town of Arita which is renowned for its pottery and adherence to traditional Japanese ways.

The Fukuoka experience had identified Seko as one of *the* men to beat in world marathoning. It had also shown that runners could produce their best times after a comparatively slow early pace and there was a lesson in the way the racing only really started after Itoh's onslaught at 30 km. When Clohessy and Rob sat down to analyse the event they were to draw conclusions that would have far-reaching effects on their strategy for major races.

Chapter Ten

Success, Italian Style

The year 1981 was to transform Rob's life. It began in a familiar enough fashion, in the block of holiday units at Falls Creek. Most of the usual gang of Melbourne runners were there and Gerard Barrett had come down from Queensland with his new wife Shane, in training for her second marathon. Barrett burnt up the mountain roads, often running by himself because he went at his long runs a bit more fiercely than the Clohessy group. In contrast, Rob was cruising in the aftermath of his marathon effort in Japan. He said, 'The Fukuoka run gave me a lot of confidence. I was very surprised to end up running 2:10:44 after my stomach trouble. Now my psychological situation is really good. The fast time has given me a boost but I've got no doubts at all that I can do even better.'

Asked about Clayton's record, he replied, 'I feel it is within reach. Anyone who gets below 2:11 has the potential to threaten the record. It's a matter of getting everything right and hoping you are the only one up there when things click into place. If you get the right set of guys in the right conditions it will go for sure. I think it will go at Fukuoka.'

Before returning to Fukuoka, Rob had two major projects for the first half of 1981: to complete the final six months of his science degree in biophysics and to compete for Australia in the IAAF cross-country championships in Madrid. Text books were shunted to one side in late March for the trip to Europe. Although his training had not returned to optimum levels for the big 11.9 km race over a heavily grassed, somewhat hilly course in the Spanish capital, he enjoyed the morale-boosting presence of Gayelene, who was a member of Australia's women's team, and of Clohessy, who was manager of the Australian party. There were a record thirty-three teams in the men's event, including for the first time squads from Ethiopia and Kenya. High placings would be more difficult to snatch than in earlier years. The usual helter-skelter start of a European cross-country event was exacerbated in Madrid by the fact that the first kilometre was straight, slightly downhill and wind-assisted. Rob could hardly have chosen a worse moment to be caught by the starter's gun as he was adjusting his singlet. He was flat-footed as the 230-plus competitors set off at a frantic sprint, with the leaders hurtling through the first kilometre in 2:35. But the young Australian ran so hard he was up with the pace-setters after only a further 500 metres. His teammates Brian Lewry, Steve Austin and John Andrews were also in the top thirty. The Ethiopians were in the lead and it was rough going as they took turns to surge away from the jostling, crowded field. Despite this Rob felt, 'It was just great to be up there, feeling good and competitive.'

Also in the leading group were the defending champion, American Craig Virgin, New Zealander Rod Dixon, Englishman Julian Goater, Portuguese Fernando Mamede, and the Ethiopians Miruts Yifter (double Olympic gold medallist), Mohammed Kedir (Olympic 10,000 m bronze medallist), Berhan Germa, Dereje Nedi and Kebede Balcha. In the middle of the fourth of five laps, the Ethiopians suddenly accelerated, sprinting out to the middle of the course and then stopping as the bell clanged. Officials shouted at them to keep running and, confused and protesting, they tried to regain their momentum. Their miscounting of the laps was expensive. They had had seven runners in the top eleven before the premature finish, but now ten outsiders were able to whisk by as they hesitated. Rob overhauled Yifter, one of the first Ethiopians to recover, as they climbed a series of hills into the last lap and then set off after the other leaders. And although Virgin, Kedir, Mamede, Goater and the hometown hero Antonio Prieto remained beyond his reach in the run home, his sixth placing marked his international breakthrough and was the best achieved by an Australian. Wardlaw described it as 'the outstanding male performance in a major event in the past decade, Rick Mitchell (the Commonwealth gold and Olympic silver medallist at 400 m) excepted.'

Australia finished fifth, its best team effort in three attempts, behind Ethiopia, the US, Kenya and Spain and ahead of such traditional cross-country powers as England and Belgium. The Australian placings and times were: de Castella, 6th, 35:20; Austin, 23rd, 35:50; Andrews, 34th, 35:59; Lewry, 49th, 36:12; Max Little, 61st, 36:20; Wardlaw, 81st, 36:30; Garry Bentley, 100th, 36:50; Robert Neylon, 171st, 37:50 and Tim O'Shaughnessy, 187th, 38:29.

In the women's race, Australia finished 16th with Anne Lord placing highest at 51st. Gayelene, still bedevilled by her knee problems, was 89th. She said, 'I was fit enough to train with Robert in the mornings before we went to Europe, but my leg was particularly bad during the tour and they were my last serious races before major surgery to correct the problem.'

The Australians moved on to Milan, Italy, to contest that other European cross-country classic, the 9.5 km Cinque Mulini. Most of Madrid's big guns were there, headed by Yifter, Kedir and the other Ethiopians who dominated again with surging front-running. Rob, looking like a titan among the slight Africans, hung on to the leaders and eventually surged himself, driving ahead of all but Kedir, until the African sprinted for the tape like a startled antelope, rounding the Australian to win by six seconds. Yifter was ten seconds behind Rob in third place and his countrymen came in fourth, fifth and sixth. The Ethiopian bloc was followed by Lewry, Italy's 5,000 m European champion Venanzio Ortis, and Austin. Andrews was 18th, Bentley 26th, O'Shaughnessy 28th, Wardlaw 30th and Little 31st for Australia to place second in the teams' race behind the amazing men from the Ethiopian plateau.

Next up was another Milanese event, the Stamilano Distance Classic over 22 km which had been dominated for years by the Ethiopians. Rob's Cinque Mulini effort had made him something of a local hero in Milan, where most people had relatives in Australia and found it natural to identify with an Australian with a Latin-sounding name. As he set off, among the Ethiopians again, there were chants of 'de Castella, de Castella'. He said, 'They really got behind me when they realized I was competitive against the Ethiopians who had dominated their road and cross-country events for years. They seemed to think of me as some sort of a Great White Hope.'

The crowd support helped him ignore a calf muscle strain and two burst blisters as he paced it with the aggressive Africans. Yifter led through 5 km in 13:36 (eight seconds faster than Rob's track best at the time) and Kedir took them through 10 km in 28:46. Rob was in front by 15 km (43:25) and had dropped all but the Africans' top marathoner, Kebede Balcha, by the time he raced through 20 km in 58:29. Balcha adopted the waiting tactics that had given him victory over another Australian, Dave Chettle, in the 1979 Montreal Marathon. He sat behind Rob until there were only 150 m left and then dashed into the lead. It seemed all over until the Australian gritted his teeth, dropped his arms and drove back past the Ethiopian with 50 m to run to win by a second in 64:52, a time which compared very well with the then usually accepted half-marathon (21.1 km) world best of 62:16.

The Australian had achieved his second breakthrough in a week with his first victory over a top-class field. Clohessy was jubilant. 'Rob's superb performances in Madrid and Milan mark the arrival of a new international star — a competitor ready now to challenge for top honours. I believe he has reached a higher stage of development and is capable of real greatness.'

That evening Rob received a standing ovation as he walked into a Milanese restaurant; his first taste of fame was not at all disagreeable. Next morning he packed his trophies, soaked his ragged soles in salt water, then immersed them in a pain-reducing ice bucket and contemplated the future. He was being hailed by the Italian press as 'the conqueror of the Ethiopian hordes'.

Back in Australia life continued as before. The conqueror shared the cooking and the washing up and teased Sue Schneider unmercifully about her accent. In between these responsibilities, Rob reflected on the business of being an international hero. There was little glamour in the work as he laboured to put away the mileage necessary to prepare properly for Fukuoka. Training was punctuated by some notable road-racing performances, particularly a 40:08 course record for Sydney's City-to-Surf race over fourteen hilly kilometres. He won the Australian 25 km road title in Perth in an unextended 74:41.4 and graduated from Swinburne Technical College to take up a job at the Australian Institute of Sport in Canberra, where he was to work as a biophysicist in a sports science laboratory.

The move to peaceful Canberra brought with it easily accessible forest paths and bush tracks for running and a job where the hours could be regulated to suit the demands of training. Work intermeshed perfectly with the exploration of human possibilities on the road. This was a vast improvement in what Clohessy called the runner's total environment. Rob's new boss was a former top-class Australian Rules footballer and cricketer, Dr Dick Telford, who was a runner himself and cherished an ambition to better 2:20 for a marathon. He and 3:55 miler Ken Hall, a student at the Institute, were ready-made training companions. The institute's administrator, Peter Bowman, once said good humouredly of the laboratory, 'I don't know what goes on over there. Every time I ring them they are out running. Even the receptionist is a runner.'

The Italians wanted to see more of Rob and invited him to compete in a mass-participation 18 km road race held in conjunction with the World Cup track and field meeting in Rome in September. Rob obliged by limping home (he had blisters and calf trouble again) through the cobbled streets of the Eternal City ahead of 15,000 other runners to win the loosely titled Marathon of History and Peace. A striking memento of the race, a big colour print of him racing alone past the Spanish Steps, was soon hanging in his home in Canberra.

He and Gayelene moved north to Brescia for the 12 km San Rocchino Grand Prix where he was to meet some of Europe's best distance men. A chance meeting in a quiet little restaurant there led them into a long-term friendship with a pair of Italian doctors. Gayelene remembers, 'Somehow we got into a conversation with Dr Sylvana Capa who is one of those people who put the fun into travelling. When I told her I had knee problems she said, "Don't worry. I have a friend, Dr Gabriel Rosa, who will help you with your knee."

'When I mentioned shopping she said, "Don't worry. I have a sister who speaks good English and will help you with your shopping."

'Then when we said we would like to get off the beaten track and have a look at the Italian countryside, she said: "Don't worry. I have a brother with a nice car and he will take you sight-seeing."

'It turned out that Dr Rosa worked at a sports institute in the city and he was proud to show Robert around it and to compare notes about the Institute of Sport in Canberra. The four of us became very close friends and we found the Italians a very pleasant contrast to some people in the running scene elsewhere who only seem interested in getting the best possible performance for the least trouble or expense.'

On race day Rob was again troubled by his blisters, but on a steep incline between the city's medieval buildings he turned on his climbing power and according to a local observer 'left the rest of the competitors looking as if they were running on a treadmill'.

He was out in front and all alone for the second half of the race and cruised home in 35:54.5, thirty seconds clear of Austrian Dittmar Millonig. Among the others stranded by his mid-race burst were West Germany's Thomas Wessinghage, Belgium's Alex Hagelsteens and Ireland's Gerry Keenan. Rob commented, 'The blisters were killing me. I got some in Rome last Sunday but these are worse. It could mean the end of my plans to run in the Maple Leaf half-marathon in New York State next weekend.'

So it was once again to the ice bucket, dear friends. And although the freezing water eased the discomfort and there was the consoling thought that 'a little pain never hurt anybody', Rob was still hobbling when he and Gayelene left the transatlantic flight in New York City and took a local connection to Vermont where a hot reception was waiting from two of the best runners on the fast-growing US road circuit. Herb Lindsay and Jon Sinclair would have found it hard to believe the Aussie stranger had blistered feet and a nagging calf problem when he led them through the first half of the hilly course at a pace that promised an unexpected US record. Rob said, 'I was running quite strongly but there was still a fair amount of discomfort. Herb and Jon got away from me and were battling it out when Jon got a stitch on one of the climbs. Herb finished with an American record 61:47, Jon clocked 62:40 and I got a PB 63:04 in third place. All things considered, I was pretty happy.'

During the following week the Australian freshened up with some easy running and what he calls 'massage runs' — very slow relaxed jogging on a yielding surface. He reasoned, 'This sort of running loosens your muscles and I prefer it to massage. I feel with massage there is a tendency for the muscles to become dependent on it and they tighten when you don't get regular treatment. You can't always have a masseur with you when you travel.'

He and his blisters were in better shape for the BMW 15 km race at

White Plains, New York, the next weekend. Soon after the start on the mansion-lined country lanes of Westchester, he bolted away from Bill Rodgers, the American folk hero, and Sydney Maree, the South African-born sub-3:50 miler. Running aggressively over the winding course's many hills, he passed 10 km in 28:56 and reached 15 km in 43:54 to break the course record by 2:55 and finish thirty-seven seconds clear of multiple Boston and New York marathon winner Rodgers. Maree was a weary third. When Clohessy heard about the run he exulted, 'That's what I like about Deek. Some front-runners lose heart when they have a defeat like that half-marathon. The next time out they just go through the motions and wait to be passed. But he came straight back and beat a strong field with an aggressive display of hill running.'

The next stop was the Pepsi Challenge 10 km in Purchase, New York, where the main danger seemed to be Canadian 5,000 m track runner Paul Williams. As it turned out there were other perils. Rob charged away at the gun with Williams hanging at his shoulder and the US Olympian Greg Fredericks battling to stay in touch. A police car was parked in a narrow side road the runners were to take, blocking it. The Australian, not familiar with the course, ran past the turn-off, then, seeing his mistake, swerved back and around the front of the car. At the same moment somebody yelled at the policeman that he was blocking the runners' right-of-way and he put his foot on the accelerator. Luckily he had good reflexes and hit the brakes just as suddenly when he saw Rob dead ahead. He screeched to a stop just behind a set of pumping legs. A less determined runner might have been unnerved, but Rob kept his concentration as well as his small gap on Williams. They went through 5 km in 14:18 and Rob gradually stretched his lead to the finish line which he crossed in 28:43. He told the crowd at the presentation: 'I'm very satisfied with the race. Being a marathoner I'm delighted to win a 10,000 m race. This is part of my build-up to Fukuoka, as all my races this year have been.'

Rob stayed around to socialize and talk with the press but the Pepsi organizers were apparently not over-impressed with his efforts on the road or afterwards. His request for some help with air fares to enable Gayelene to visit Sue Schneider, who had returned to America, on their way back to their international connection in Los Angeles was turned down. It would have amounted to about $300 and seemed a small request when many American athletes were collecting thousands just to turn up at races.

Rob's American successes strengthened his thesis that US road runners were made to seem a little larger than life by all the whiz-bang publicity churned out by magazines dependent on the North American running scene for their existence. He had said earlier in the year, before injuries began to water down Australia's distance-running strength: 'It would be good to take an Australian squad to America. We could sell ourselves as a sort of package attraction and I think we would blow the Americans off the road. Fukuoka is often an illustration of the relative standards, with the top Americans not doing as well as our best runners.'

However, American running was on the eve of one of its proudest moments. Rob was no sooner back among the treadmills and human-performance gadgetry of his Canberra science laboratory than news came through that Alberto Salazar, 23, had broken Derek Clayton's world record of twelve years' standing by running 2:08:13 in the point-to-point New York Marathon. Salazar, a former schoolboy prodigy who had once run himself close to death to win a race in a heatwave, had promised weeks before his second marathon start that he would break the record. He proved a man of his word.

Rob's reaction was typically positive. 'Salazar has done us all a favour,' he said. 'Clayton's time had stood for so long we had started to think of it, unfairly, as a fairytale. Had he really run that fast? Could anyone else ever do it? Now Salazar has brought that sort of performance within reach. The new record is there. It's more tangible.'

He agreed Salazar was a brave and talented runner, but added as an afterthought, 'I'd be interested to know how he recovers from this.'

The Australian had restricted his running on his first week home to 150 gentle kilometres. Now as his battered legs and feet recovered from his overseas tour and Salazar's record and the proximity of Fukuoka combined to build up his motivation, he began to boost his mileage and increase its quality. Interviewed at this time by a reporter who contended that a prerequisite for distance running was insanity, he said, 'You don't have to be mad — but it helps. Sometimes when I'm running through the rain and cold and people drive past in the comfort of their cars, I think maybe I'm getting myself nowhere except to the pneumonia ward. I can never let my hair down. It's essential to have nine or ten hours sleep each night and I have to be careful what I eat. What you eat is what your body runs on and you can't afford to forget that.'

In spite of these almost-negative thoughts, Rob was soon back on the training trails. Surprised by the speed of his recovery from such a hard series of races, he was soon up to normal mileage. He planned a 48 km run through the Stromlo Forest in November as the climax of the heavy phase of his preparation for the Fukuoka race on the first Sunday in December. Gayelene, who had hobbled bravely through a less extreme workout, was waiting as he strode over the final few metres. He was moving easily, his face was split by a wolfish grin and his eyes alight with anticipation.

Then, as a speed tune-up, he went to Melbourne to take on the national champion, Steve Austin, over his own 5,000 m speciality. Rob did no special track preparation for the club event but he led most of the distance and surged in an effort to shake Austin off with 500 m to go. When the track specialist hung on and then passed the marathoner with 300 m left, the contest seemed to be over. But Rob dropped his arms and drove himself up the straight to win by a stride in 13:35, a career best by almost five seconds. Clohessy enthused, 'He outkicked a virtual four-minute miler (in fact, Austin ran 3:57:7 later that season). There's a lot of psychology in finishing. If a runner believes he can kick, then he can kick. Rob has that belief now.'

The waiting and the fine-tuning were over. Rob and Gayelene collected their documentation for the journey to Japan and, unconsciously at least, he began weighing the possibilities of a world record. He said, 'I think some of them will go out after it. I'm hoping to be pretty competitive, but to win I'd have to run faster than I ever have before ...'

CHAPTER ELEVEN

Joining The Giants

The day before Fukuoka '81, the five Australians competing in the race were called to a press conference along with the other 111 competitors from thirteen nations. Selected runners were asked their predicted time for the race, their choice as winner and how they fancied their own chances. The Russian Vladimir Kotov was close to the consensus when he answered, 'I think the winning time will be between 2:09 and 2:10 and a Japanese runner will win.' The new Australian marathon champion, Garry Bentley, was one of the last to be interviewed and the only runner to give an aggressively different answer. Despite three previous years of Japanese monopoly on the top three places, he predicted, 'The marathon will be won in between 2:09 and 2:10, but you can forget about a Japanese runner winning, because an Australian will.' He was not quite optimistic enough.

Rob wanted his usual pre-race meal of nourishing complex carbohydrates that evening, but found there were cultural complications. The Japanese scorned brown rice, despite the extra nutrients in the husks. The less nourishing but universally approved white rice was all that was available in his hotel or in nearby restaurants. In case of just such an emergency, he had brought along his own supply of brown rice and wholemeal noodles and he and Gayelene joined the Italian contingent at a small restaurant in a side street where the owner said he was willing to cook a carbo-load dinner. Rob had been invited by the Italian runner Pier Giovanni Poli and his coach Dr

Gabriel Rosa, whom he had met in Milan earlier in the year. Gayelene recalled, 'When we arrived at the restaurant we were surprised to see it had been shut for the evening, so we were being entertained as a private party. Rob handed the food over and they cooked the lot, not just part of it as we expected. Rob had a great mountain of food on his plate and the owner and his family were amazed. They feed brown rice to animals in Japan and they couldn't believe that was all he was eating. The people couldn't speak English but they were just so obliging. They wouldn't charge for their cooking and gave us each a beautifully wrapped little present before we left. Mine was a silk purse and Rob's was a tie and handkerchief.'

The race began in cool, cloudy weather at noon the next day, 6 December. There were 50,000 people along the route, many of them waving the traditional small paper flags.

Start to 5 km

Fukuoka's usual big, fast, leading pack went careering out of Heiwadai Stadium with foreigners well to the fore. It was like the old Dandenong days for Rob as he bowled along in the company of Dave Chettle who had come from England in the hope of achieving a second elusive sub-2:11 on the course where he had set his PB 2:10:20 six years earlier. They went through the 5 km together in 15:31 with Lawrie Whitty and Rob Wallace five seconds slower and Garry Bentley another three seconds back.

5 km to 10 km

The American Garry Bjorklund had resolved before the race to go to the front and push for a world record as soon as the pace dropped below 15:30 per 5 km. The bearded American was as good as his word even at this early stage and as he warmed up to a 2:08 tempo the pack started to shed members. Among the Japanese who stayed up there were the tiny Kunimitsu Itoh, the third place getter in 1980 and a man with impressive track credentials, and the taller, bespectacled Shigeru Soh, who had finished fifth the previous year. Rob lost his running mate as Chettle found the fifteen-minute/5 km pace a bit too willing. By the second feeding table the Tasmanian had dropped thirteen seconds behind and was heading for an unhappy 2:20-plus day. Whitty had dropped half a minute and Bentley and Wallace, running together, had opted for the second division.

10 km to 15 km

The pain started early. Rob's feet felt hot and then began to blister. He said, 'It began just before 10 km and there was the fear of what the pain would be like after another 30 km. I tried altering my foot placement to ease it but when that didn't work I just concentrated on shutting it out of my mind. You can't afford negative thoughts in a marathon.' He maintained his rhythm behind Bjorklund's even pace-setting. The other Australians were falling back, with Whitty the closest but almost fifty seconds behind the leaders at the 15 km drink table, which Rob reached in 45:29.

15 km to 20 km

More steady running and the pain receded. After 16 km his feet were numb. He looked at the splits he had written on his hand and was surprised to see the pace was better than world record level. At each feeding station he had a couple of mouthfuls of a diluted glucose-water mixture developed for him by Dick Telford, his colleague at the Institute of Sport.

20 km to 25 km

The pack was now trimmed to six with Bjorklund rounding the halfway turnabout a stride ahead of Soh. Rob was sixth around in a tight bunch in a time of 1:03:48, just forty-five seconds slower than his PB for the half-marathon distance. Shigeru Soh's twin brother Takeshi, second in 1980, and the Italian Poli were not far behind the leaders, but Whitty, now the closest of the other Australians, was two minutes ten seconds in arrears.

25 km to 30 km

The last 15 km had passed in a quick, even forty-five minutes and disposed of dual Olympic champion Waldemar Cierpinski of East Germany, who withdrew with a leg injury. Deek commented, 'Bjorklund did all the work until about 25 km, then he put in a bit of a surge. We went over to the drinks table, he took off and opened about seventy to eighty metres on us. Once we got a group together we finally began to peg him back. When we caught him he just really folded. There was myself, Soh (Shigeru) and Itoh. Soh dropped off and Itoh was sitting right behind me and I thought: "Oh hell, here we go. He's just going to sit on me."'

What a team! Pat Clohessy, Rob and Gayelene share the emotional spoils after his Brisbane Commonwealth Games triumph.

The prince and the pretender take tea together before their confrontation on the roads of Rotterdam. The prince, world record-holder Alberto Salazar, is second from left, flanked by his masseur, Ilpo. World one-hour record-holder and Rotterdam Marathon organizer Jos Hermans is in the centre with his wife Bepke, while Rob is surrounded by members of the Clews clan, Graham and Gayelene.

The king and queen of the marathon world: Rob de Castella and Greta Waitz train together in Oslo before winning World Championship crowns in Helsinki in 1983.

30 km to 35 km

The Australian led through 30 km in 1:31:09 with the little Japanese tucked in behind. Deek's confidence grew. 'I started to hear him puff and thought, "That's a good sign." At the hill at 32 km I put in a bit of a surge and he just dropped off. Next time I looked around I just couldn't see him.' The 5 km split took only 14:59 and as he passed 35 km in 1:31:09 he was fifteen seconds clear of Itoh.

35 km to 40 km

The Australian was running alone now, beginning to feel the strain. Victory was virtually beyond doubt and as the aching exhaustion mounted, his pace dropped to 15:24 for the 5 km. He said, 'With 5 km to go I let my mind drift. I thought, "What a thrill if I win this." The next thing I knew I was stumbling. I thought I had lifted my legs but I only imagined I had. From there it was a matter of concentrating on every stride.' A few English-speaking fans shouted to him to 'go for the record', but he thought they were referring to Derek Clayton's course record of 2:09:37 rather than Salazar's world mark. Itoh held himself together but could make no impression on the Australian's lead.

40 km to Finish

Rob only realized how fast he was running after he re-entered the stadium. Among the cloudburst of noise beating down on him he heard a familiar voice. Gayelene was shouting desperately: 'Go for the world record, go for the world record!'

Somehow he forgot the weariness and dredged up a final driving sprint to complete the last 400 m in sixty-eight seconds and finish in 2:08:18; with Salazar's time just a tantalising five seconds beyond reach.

His reaction was positive. 'I wasn't at all disappointed. I hadn't even thought of Salazar's time. It was just a big thrill to dominate the race. It's the fastest Fukuoka, which to me is about the same thing as the world's fastest. Nearly every top marathoner in history has run that course and to take 1:19 off Clayton's record is pretty awesome.'

Itoh came in second in a PB 2:09:37, matching almost to the second Clayton's 1967 course record, and after him the finishing order was: 3 Shigeru Soh, Japan, 2:10:19; 4 Poli, Italy, 2:11:19; 5 Takeshi Soh, Japan, 2:11:29; 6 Garry Bjorklund, US, 2:11:35; 7 Tommy Persson, Sweden, 2:12:19; 8 Vladimir Kotov, USSR, 2:12:25; 9 Domingo

Tibaduiza, Colombia, 2:13:04; 10 Art Boileau, Canada, 2:13:31 and 11 Paul Ballinger, NZ, 2:14:04.

Whitty was 15th in 2:14:15, Bentley 24th in 2:16:18, Wallace 25th in 2:16:43 and Chettle 41st in 2:20:03.

When I rang Rob from Sydney that night the pain, almost mystically, had vanished from memory. He said, 'I felt really strong in the last 10 km and only got tired in the last kilometre.' He laughed about the five-second shortfall. 'Only five seconds! I wonder what part of the race I lost that in.'

Asked how he felt, he replied, 'Great! It might be a bit different when the euphoria wears off, but at the moment I really feel good.'

Gayelene was amazed at his after-race recovery, saying, 'After he ran across the line he kept telling me how easy it had been.' And that provided a glimpse of the mental strength of the man who has shaken the marathon world. As he once said: 'You can't afford negative thoughts in a marathon.'

There had been something close to public dismay in Japan when three-time winner Toshihiko Seko decided not to start. Some claimed it was because of a leg injury and other reports said he was skipping the race because it didn't fit into his build-up for the 1984 Olympics. Rob told the after-race press conference, 'I really wish Seko had been there. I would like to have run against him because he is one of the very best marathoners in the world.' Later, he also expressed disappointment about Salazar's absence.

The news of his achievement shook the Melbourne running community. Chris Wardlaw described that Sunday night for *Australian Runner* magazine: 'Don the Groundsman (a local identity) phoned me at 5:08 p.m. "I've just got the result. First Deek 2:08:18. Gotta ring a few people." I still don't know how he beat me to the result. I tried to phone Pat Clohessy. He was possessed [engaged]. Tim O'Shaughnessy was at a barbecue. He tried to ring Pat who was engaged. And me, engaged. He said to Marion, his spouse: "It must be a big one. The phones are running hot." I counted up the fifteen phone calls (no embellishment, but admittedly three were with Pat!) I had that night. All I could say was "unbelievable, incredible etc." '

Rob's run was the fastest achieved on an out-and-back course and many statisticians would regard it as the world's best. Salazar's five-second advantage lost what little significance it deserved, in Australian eyes at least, when you considered it was a point-to-point effort favoured by a tailwind and assisted by a pacing vehicle equipped with a digital clock to keep the leading runners aware of elapsed time. By comparison, the Australian had to run in the dark as far as progressive times were concerned, with no assistance from the terrain and he had had to consider the tactical challenges of an immensely stronger field.

Amid all the interviews, back-slapping and conversations with marathon promoters during that evening in Fukuoka, Rob received a telegram from the great track runner Ron Clarke, breaker of eighteen world records in the 1960s, who was recovering from heart surgery in Melbourne. It said: 'You are the greatest athlete Australia has produced.'

In the hotel that night Vladimir Kotov produced a bottle of good Russian vodka and Rob got just a little drunk.

Up to this time, most of his achievements had gone unnoticed in Australia, with only people involved in running appreciating the high quality of his best performances or his awesome potential. But Fukuoka was front-page news. The *Australian* newspaper's report on the Monday morning after the race carried a few paragraphs that were to spark a seven-day sensation in the media. 'Commercial sponsors will now leap at the chance to have the Australian [de Castella] endorse their products in the booming marathon sport which supports a million-dollar world circuit. Salazar had a contract for $1 million dangled before him in the wake of his world record.'

Within the next few days the staid old *Sydney Morning Herald* carried headlines saying 'Marathon man is real hot property' and, over a picture highlighting his tattered soles, 'Feet worth a fortune'. Jim Webster, who knows a great deal about track and field, wrote: 'The leading track promoters were all at Fukuoka last Sunday . . . and they were queueing afterwards to try to get the Australian to run for them. He received eleven invitations on the spot for other marathons and they would all have been offering lucrative expenses — the replacement word for money in the tainted world of amateur athletics. I learned from a reliable source that one American promoter was offering to pay de Castella $US15,000 just to turn up at his meeting and would pay him another $14,000 if he won, $12,000 if he came second, $10,000 for third, and so on.' Another *Herald* reporter, Tim Dare, an able journalist but less familiar with the world of top-level running, thought he had uncovered a major scandal. His page one story began, a bit breathlessly, 'The marathon runner Robert de Castella, an Olympic representative and now Australia's top athlete, revealed yesterday that he receives payment from a leading sports shoe manufacturer. De Castella said Adidas meets all his travelling expenses, training expenses, gives him a small living allowance and provides him with running shoes. He competes in Adidas running shoes.'

Dare had obviously not heard of the International Amateur Athletic Federation's tentative efforts to come to terms with the twentieth century and, especially, the complicated world of US road racing with its under-the-table payments, over-the-table payments, trust funds, sports clothes empires and running millionaires. Somebody like Bill Rodgers, who had amassed a real fortune out of running, would have found Dare's claim that his interview 'blew the lid off shamateurism' a little droll. Rob, forthright as his own racing tactics, said, 'I think if I wanted to capitalize on it fully, the best thing would be to go to the States now, and probably I could pick up $150,000 a year. The whole amateur thing is very up in the air. Strictly speaking I am not allowed to get anything, so I am not prepared to say in print what I get. All the top runners in the world are getting paid a lot to wear shoes and do endorsements. Everybody knows it, but it's a matter of proving it. The Americans get the most directly. The Europeans don't get any cash, but they get a house, a car and don't have to do any work.'

Dare took these revelations to the executive director of the Amateur Athletic Union of Australia, Rick Pannell, who said there was confusion over just how much 'assistance' was allowed under the IAAF's liberalized rules on amateurism. But he told Dare there would be an investigation if any amateur athlete received unauthorized contributions. The next day, in a *Herald* follow-up, Pannell very sensibly told Dare he would not be launching any witch-hunts.

In the wash-up from all this fuss, Rob was approached by the International Management Group of America, Mark McCormack's US-based organization which has vast experience in looking after the business interests of such sporting celebrities as Wimbledon tennis champions John Newcombe and Evonne Cawley and international golfer Jan Stephenson. After talks with Graeme Hannan in Sydney and Drew Mearns, head of the organization's running division, in

Cleveland, Rob agreed to hand the business side of being an international sporting hero over to IMG. He said, 'It's a matter of specialization. I'm a runner. They are businessmen. They protect me from the hassles and I'm very happy with the arrangement.'

Ironically, the US arm of IMG had another marathon runner on its books, a fellow called Alberto Salazar.

CHAPTER TWELVE

Fukuoka Fallout

A month after this remarkable triumph, Rob was back into his training routine and at work at the Institute of Sport. Annoyingly, not everything had reverted to normal. The blisters on his feet had healed but the effort that had seemed almost easy in the post-race excitement had left other, deeper scars. His heartbeat was still elevated; he was affected by allergies he had not known before. He had a series of colds and occasional headaches. In the depths of this post-race physical depression, the telephone rang. It was sports writer Richard Sleeman looking for a story and such was the timing of the call that the worried runner poured out his problems. Sleeman wrote in the *Australian:* 'The feeling is one of prolonged hangover, though de Castella rarely touches alcohol, and certainly not to excess in any one session. Despite the congratulations that have been justifiably heaped on him since his return and the hearty cheers of well-wishers, de Castella is suffering regularly from periods of depression. He admitted being testy with his wife, Gayelene, and with close friends and family, although he is among the most congenial and approachable of the top Australian sportsmen. So much has the effort of 6 December taken out of him, almost without de Castella being aware of it, that the thing which has always been paramount in his life — running — is suddenly a chore ... in the calm of his work, de Castella normally has a distance runner's low pulse rate of forty to the minute, or less. Now it's more than fifty. De

Castella expects the depression and illness to last another month or so.'

In his determination to cope with and overcome his problems, Rob had previously kept the details to himself. The article surprised Clohessy who immediately concluded that Sleeman had caught the runner in an unusually low moment. Gayelene missed the article and when I mentioned the range of her husband's self-confessed problems, she was equally surprised.

As he battled to complete his usual weekly training schedule (about 250 km of running plus hours of exercise, at this stage) and to regain some form, Rob organized a 10,000 m track race in Canberra in a bid to improve his best for the distance from 28:16:2 to below twenty-eight minutes. Top-line Australians at the distance, Gerard Barrett from Brisbane and Andrew Lloyd from Sydney, came down to give him support and incentive and, in the event, pushed him back to third place. His time was twenty seconds below his best and some heads began to shake.

Had the Fukuoka effort burned him out? Precedents were not hard to find for a runner leaving some indefinable part of himself on the road where he had appeared to have his finest, and most promising, hour. Derek Clayton's second world record at Antwerp in 1969 had left him physically shattered with symptoms of internal damage that no doctor could explain. He was never to be an international force again. This case was stark and dramatic, but there were other examples of a more subtle toll imposed on a man who pushes through 42.2 km at a tempo close to 15:10 for each 5 km. Other young runners had made prodigious breakthroughs and appeared on the brink of even greater things but had never run as effectively again. Briton Ian Thompson had completed scores of marathons in his eight-year career, but his best time remained that of his second race, 2:09:12. Chettle ran 2:10:20 in his second international marathon and hadn't matched that since. Even Cierpinski of the twin gold medals has to look back over eight years of extensive competition to his best effort of 2:09:55. It was as if newcomers found the long, painful road easier to travel. Its realities, once explored, became an extra burden for some athletes to carry. Clayton (before Salazar and de Castella fully emerged) once explained it this way. 'After my 2:08:33, I couldn't have run that way again. This is why I think that a person who is going to break the record is a person who is going to come down from

2:16 or 2:17 and do a 2:08. I came down from 2:18 to 2:09. Bill Rodgers came down from 2:18 to 2:09. Ron Hill has done that. Nijboer has done that. I'll tell you the reason this happens. A 2:18 or 2:17 is expected of us. It's not a real tough run. It's just a hurdle that we overcome to get down to fast times. Once you get under 2:10 you know what that takes out of you. No one runs under 2:10 and finds it easy, no one. And you know what you've got to do to run faster. So, if you run 2:09:30 you think, "Hell, the effort I put into the 2:09:30, how am I going to run a minute faster?" You can't conceive it in your own mind . . . the effort it took out of me to run 2:08:33, I was blown. There was no way, mentally, I could get myself up again to go and try to beat that time. I was finished. That was it.'

So the doubters wondered. Would Rob be handicapped by memories of Fukuoka's aftermath when the competitive pressures came on again?

Sure in the faith of gradual physical adaptation, Clohessy expressed no such fears. The years and kilometres invested in converting Rob into the most efficient running machine in history would not be wasted. He had to come through or all the common-sense, the intelligent theories tested with decades of experience, would be proved worthless. Clohessy was confident. 'He had a few problems but I wasn't worried. There were a lot of invitations after Fukuoka and I think he accepted a few too many. He's a big runner who burns up a lot of energy. If he doesn't get ten hours sleep a night his training and his performances fall off.'

Others, of course, expressed less faith as the runner left for Rome to compete in the IAAF Cross-Country Championship for a third time. Gayelene went to Italy with Rob and considered his prospects with concern. 'After we came back from Fukuoka I thought "He's really going to be pushing it this year." I knew before we went to Rome that he was nowhere nearly ready for such a tough event. During the race he had it written all over his face. It was hard all the way; a real chore. At times like that it worries me watching him race. As a runner I now what he is going through. He can take so much out of his body. He utilizes everything. It's a bit frightening.'

The race was dominated by Alberto Salazar, then 23. It was the first meeting between the two young men whose destinies were to be so intertwined. The front-running American led for most of the 12 km race but lost out in the final metres to a whippet-like sprint from the tiny Ethiopian Mohammed Kedir. Rob struggled along in about fifteenth position and pushed his way grimly through the field to finish tenth. It was a solid enough performance, but there was no sparkle. It was not quite enough to kill off all the doubts.

The second biggest event of the European cross-country season was the Cinque Mulini, where Rob had placed second in 1981 behind Kedir. This time he went to the starting line with a cold. Gayelene remarked, 'After an effort like the Rome race, a runner's body is drained and his resistance down. Rob caught the bug from me but refused to pull out or to tell anybody about it in case they thought he was offering it as an excuse. While I had it I could scarcely jog.'

Rob followed home Ethiopia's Eshutu Tura, Italy's Alberto Cova, Britain's Mike McLeod and Kedir to take fifth place, but in spite of his illness he managed to outrun such big names as New Zealand's Rod Dixon and the East Germans Werner Schildhauer and Hans-Jorg Kunze, three of the nine men who had beaten him in Rome. 'The defeats are good for him,' said Clohessy, quite seriously. 'They help to keep his feet on the ground, and he reacts pretty well to them.'

The next event of his programme was a lot closer to Rob's area of specialization, the annual Stramilano Distance Classic in Milan. As the winner over 22 km in 1981 and conqueror of the 'Ethiopian hordes', the Australian was a popular favourite with the Italians lining the route, now trimmed to the 21.1 km half-marathon distance. He set off as if the event belonged to him. As Gayelene followed on a motorcycle, he pounded into the lead at the start and went past 10 km faster than he had managed to race just that distance in Canberra only two weeks previously. His pace made the usual approach to half-marathons look decidedly faint-hearted and the crowd reacted warmly. Gayelene said, 'As I rode along I could hear the people chanting his name. They really love him over there. He said after the race that it had helped lift him along.'

As Clohessy predicted, Deek was reacting well to his defeats. By the last kilometre he had strung out such redoubtable runners as Ethiopia's double Olympic gold medallist Miruts Yifter, Cinque Mulini winner Tura and top British marathoner Bernie Ford. Gaps as wide as a minute separated the leading runners and only the jockey-like Kedir, the Olympic 10,000 m bronze medallist, was still with the Australian. And, as he did to Salazar in the IAAF race, the African outsprinted his rival in the final few hundred metres to take the top prize. As a bonus, he collected a world record set up by Rob's bold pace-setting. Kedir's time was a sensational 1:01:02 and Rob's effort of 1:01:18 was also inside the old mark.

So it was time to shelve the burn-out theories and for Australians to look forward to the Commonwealth Games marathon. Ever the perfectionist, Rob told his wife he was considering cancelling a later race engagement because — after running a world record — he didn't think he was fit enough. She said: 'I knew how tired he was. But I told him, "I know what you mean, but really, who would believe it?"'

A few days later Rob had his first win of the tour, beating the speedy Italian, Cova, in a 7.4 km Golden Shoe Road Race in the northern Italian town of Vigevano. His time eclipsed the race record set by the phenomenal British miler Steve Ovett. Cova's defeat meant Rob had turned the tables on six of the nine runners who had finished ahead of him in that weary IAAF race. Promoters swooped to sign him to compete in a one-hour track run in Rome where an attack had been promised on the seven-year-old world record for this rather esoteric event. In an hour race, dimensions are inverted with runners charging around a track for a certain time rather than over a certain distance. The bell, which usually signals the final lap, tolls instead at the beginning of the sixtieth minute. Among top-liners, the event usually includes a preliminary skirmish at the 20 km point when runners sprint to get the best time for that distance and then struggle to regain their breaths for the final two laps or so. The record in question was a distance of 20.944 km achieved by Dutchman Jos Hermens in Papendal in 1975. Hermens had also claimed the 20 km record, passing that distance in 57:24.2. They were formidable marks achieved with the help of elaborate pace-making by a team of runners who took turns to tow Hermens for a few laps before dropping to a jog and waiting to help out again after he had lapped them. The likeable Dutchman managed two consecutive 10,000 m splits in about 28:40 each.

On a windy Roman night with no pacing assistance, such a formidable record was well beyond reach, but once again Rob found himself lifted along by the enthusiastic support of an Italian crowd. After his hard spell of racing, he stepped on to the track without any special motivation. The chants of 'de Castella, de Castella' set the adrenalin flowing and he bolted away from all his pursuers to set a new Australian and Commonwealth record of 20.516 km, the sixth best mark in history. He was already well clear of the pack when he passed the 20 km marker in 58:37.2 to become history's fourth fastest runner over that distance. Among those left in his wake were a European marathon champion and an Olympic steeplechase finalist.

As usual, one of the young runner's first reactions after success overseas was to telephone Clohessy. The school teacher was cock-a-hoop with the news. 'I had sent a telegram telling him not to knock himself about. It can be mentally punishing belting about the same track fifty times and I didn't want him to drain himself. But he said it felt really easy. After a slow start on this tour, Robert has raced right back into top shape. He has raced five times in four weeks in Italy and proved he has completely recovered from Fukuoka.'

Clohessy sounded as if he had stepped out from under a cloud. Even if it was one whose existence he had refused to accept.

Following the European tour, the runner and his coach mapped out their build-up towards the Commonwealth Games with meticulous care. The offers of instant wealth from North America failed completely to deflect them from the single-minded pursuit of their major goals: Commonwealth and then Olympic gold medals and the establishment of Rob de Castella as 'not arguably, but quite clearly, the best marathon runner of our era'.

Rob returned to the familiar roads and pine forest trails around Canberra, to built up the quiet, glamourless kilometres that alone would make it all possible. Those hours, days and months of endless sweat and muscle aches were a world remote from flashbulbs, press conferences and screaming crowds. But this world, rather than that of highpoints and climactic excitement, was the one the runner normally inhabited during the ten most important years of his athletic life. In those quiet times, between the hurly-burly of competition, Clohessy and Rob worked to forge a physical and mental armoury strong enough to overcome every other marathon runner in the world.

Training can become boring without the motivation of competition, so the lead-up to Brisbane was punctuated with a scattering of races. First, there would be the Australian cross-country championship in Hobart, Tasmania, in May, then a series of short, fast races in hot weather in the United States which also would give Rob a chance to assess Boulder, Colorado, as a possible training base for the Los Angeles Olympics in 1984. A couple of races back in

Australia would finish the sharpening process.

The prospects for Brisbane were boosted when the AAU granted Rob an exemption from the marathon trial to be run over the Games course in July, less than three months before the big event. 'One of my reasons for asking for the exemption,' Rob explained, 'was that I knew I would be running shorter races in the States. There would have been a definite conflict running a marathon immediately afterwards. Another reason is that anyone running a marathon trial a few weeks before the Commonwealth Games cannot possibly perform at his best when he needs to. A marathon is different from any other event. The preparation and strategy are paramount to winning. I felt my world standing was enough to justify my selection for Australia.'

The exemption generated its own controversy when Lawrie Whitty, who had beaten a good international field over a very hilly course to win the Seoul Marathon in South Korea earlier in the year, argued that he should be exempted too. But Whitty's time in Seoul was only in the 2:14 range (although Allison Roe, who won the women's section, said his effort was worth 2:10 on a fast course) and the AAU felt he wasn't far enough ahead of his rivals to justify an exemption. Whitty promptly announced he would boycott the trial and leave the officials to make up their own minds whether they selected him or not. He stated, 'The Commonwealth Games isn't such a big deal anyway,' and no doubt he was right as far as the world at large was concerned. But the Empire and Commonwealth meetings had always ranked close behind the Olympics in importance to most Australian athletes. When Australians talked of 'Games medals' they referred to Commonwealth as well as Olympic honours. Athletes from Britain might place as much, if not more, importance on the European Championships but Australians had no such non-Commonwealth distractions. It was traditionally just as difficult to win a place in a Commonwealth as an Olympic Games squad. It depended upon the year in which you were at your peak. Rob agreed with the general feeling. 'People ask you why you are aiming for the Commonwealth Games when the marathon won't be such a big one, but the Commonwealth Games have always been something special for me. It might not be worth too many points in regard to a world ranking but you grow up hoping to compete in a Games team and the honour is more important than winning some more highly rated race like New York or Boston. And, besides, it's being run in Australia.'

No doubt the selection dispute helped Whitty's motivation for the Australian cross-country title in Hobart, but few people expected him to turn the tables on Rob who had not lost a national cross-country race since he fell and finished ninth in Brisbane in 1977. In Hobart, Rob went straight into the lead in the first of the twelve kilometres, followed by a bare-footed Whitty and the promising young Victorian newcomer, Rod O'Connor. By the 7 km mark it was a two-man contest and at 8 km Whitty surprised everyone by opening a twenty metre break from a straining de Castella. Whitty extended his lead with inspired running up a final hill and finished with arms stretched above his head and eyes squeezed shut in pure bliss. O'Connor was third and Nick de Castella came through strongly to take fourth place, his best in a senior national championship. 'Just keep your eye on young Nick,' Clohessy said later.

Big brother went back to Canberra and continued to soak up the kilometres. Then to sharpen up for his American racing, he went to Perth to run in the West Australian 25 km Road Championship, a distance that has always suited him. The result was a stunner. He came home in a scorching PB 1:14:13.6. Only American recordholder Herb Lindsay, with 1:14:09, had run faster on roads and it wasn't too far behind the track world record for the same distance, 1:13:55.8, set by Toshihiko Seko the previous year in an orchestrated race in ideal conditions in Christchurch, NZ.

The US road circuit, with its glamour and hype, was a long way from the athletic backwoods of Hobart and Perth, but it proved quite a happy hunting ground. Rob liked the look of Boulder. 'There were a lot of American athletes training at a camp there. I'm thinking of living there for six months to get acclimatized and to use the altitude to strengthen my breathing. The setting is magnificent with the city at 5,500 ft altitude and easily accessible running trails through the forests at more than 6,000 ft. If you want, you can run up to 8,000 or even 10,000 ft above sea level. So it's an ideal place for altitude training. I was very impressed.'

His first race was a seven-mile (about 11.2 km) event in Davenport, Iowa, with America's two pre-Salazar folk heroes, Frank Shorter and Bill Rodgers, heading the field. The Australian didn't fool around. He opened a twenty second break before 2 km and

Shorter said, 'When I saw that I thought: "The son-of-a-gun is going to take it from the start." That's about as good a performance as you're going to see.' Rob extended his lead steadily on a tough, hilly out-and-back course to cut more than a minute from the race record as Rodgers trailed in second and Shorter finished third. Rob described his next race, in Minneapolis, as 'low-key' but he ran the 10 km journey in 28:45 to beat a field of 2,500 and set another race record. His third engagement, the Maggie Valley Moonlight Race in North Carolina, was a little short, at 8 km, and there were some real speedsters in the field. In the end, he followed home the moonlit shadows of two-time world cross-country champion Craig Virgin and Commonwealth Games medallist (silvers for the 5,000 m and 10,000 m in 1978) Mike Musyoki to take third place. It had taken good performances to edge him out. Virgin's 22:47 was a US five-mile record and the Australian's 22:52 was also inside the old mark.

Before flying home, Rob had a good look at the Los Angeles Olympic course and concluded: 'It's going to be tough. The first 26 km is mostly slightly downhill, nice and fast, but the final 10 km is steadily uphill.'

Back home there was the Australian 25 km Road Championship to provide a final road-racing tune-up for the Big One. It was run on a smoggy, dispiriting course through the ugly Sydney industrial suburb of Botany. It was windy and Rob, experimenting with a new pair of shoes as well as a slow early pace, lifted a toenail. But he won in 1:17:01.3 from South Australian Grenville Wood and the Canberra-based New Zealander Derek Froude. Nick de Castella came in fifth and Rob's brother-in-law, Graham Clews, completed the family feeling by galloping home in tenth place.

The day after the race, Rob had an impacted wisdom tooth removed and then went back to his forest trails and roads around Canberra. His count-down had begun.

Contention continued over the selection of Australia's other two marathon entrants. The trial race (and Australian Marathon Championship) over the Games course in Brisbane was won by a Japanese, Fukiaki Abe, 23, in 2:15:56. Rob Wallace, 31, a Victorian computer programmer who had spent four years living in the US, was second in 2:16:02 and Adelaide draftsman Grenville Wood, 27, was third in 2:16:22. After the race, the selectors named Wallace as their second Games runner but left the third position open. Two months later when Whitty qualified for the overall Games squad by winning the 10,000 track trial, he was given the third marathon spot. Wood was less than happy and subsequent events gave support to his case.

Rob went to Brisbane for the track trials and found himself alone at the 5,000 m starting line with Sydney runner John Andrews. Rob recalled, 'It was a strange race. Because of withdrawals through injuries and illness, there were just the two of us. John had to win to make the team because he had not bettered the qualifying standard previously. So I was in the situation of running against somebody I didn't really want to beat. In the event he ran very well and outkicked me at the end.'

It seemed the victory was a psychological breakthrough for Andrews who finished seventh at the Games and later became a dominant force on the Australian track scene.

CHAPTER THIRTEEN

The Day Of Deek

Gayelene was especially attentive to her husband on 7 October 1982. It was a pleasant spring evening in sub-tropical Brisbane and the city was settling into a mood of cheery self-congratulation. The 1982 Commonwealth Games, now drawing to a close, had been an unqualified success. Brisbane had surprised the world and, more particularly, its own hard-bitten citizenry with the efficiency, style and friendliness of its biggest community enterprise. But there was something else in the air that Thursday evening: anticipation and excitement over sport's new glamour event, the marathon, scheduled to get under way at 6 o'clock the next morning. Gayelene noted that Rob was 'pretty keyed up', scarcely surprising because she too was worried and apprehensive. Most Australians expected the 25-year-old biophysicist to win the gold medal, yet they knew nothing of the problems he had faced in the run-up to the big event. He had come to the Games city feeling rundown, tired and with an irritated spinal disc.

The couple had moved house in Canberra about four weeks earlier and the back trouble had begun, apparently, as a strain from shifting furniture. It had worsened after an otherwise encouraging 48 km run and he was in such discomfort he had to stop training for two days and endure the mental stress of a further two days on sharply reduced mileage. He had daily physiotherapy at the Institute of Sport and borrowed a back brace to wear on a 26 km Sunday run through the

Acknowledging the applause after his Helsinki victory. 'Once I was inside the stadium, I just indulged in the emotion and satisfaction of taking out my first World Championship.' (Photograph: Chris Smith)

On his way, at last, to victory in the Cinque Mulini, Deek leads future World Champion Alberto Cova (left) at 10,000 m and Englishman Mike McLeod (right) during the 1983 race.

Stromlo Forest. He had been scheduled to sharpen up with a 5,000 m track race in Melbourne but Clohessy advised him to forget it. The coach said, 'I told him just to jog around a bit in Canberra and to have a hit-out on the roads with Ken Hall.' Rob felt as if the nightmare of his over-done Olympic year training had come back to haunt him. Had he lost his edge once again at a time when he needed to be at an absolute peak? Gaylene said, 'He seemed just as fatigued as when he really struggled and worked his butt off just to finish tenth in the World Cross-country in March.'

Burgeoning commitments as a sports celebrity meant insufficient rest to compensate for his heavy mileages. Clohessy was furious. 'Rob told me he'd been on aeroplanes on nineteen days of the past month. I hit the roof. I warned him he would have to ease off or he would throw away the whole thing.' A few weeks before the Games, Rob found it necessary to say 'enough' to media representatives wanting interviews. He said, 'I was tired, and sensitive to the fact that I was tired.' There was some reassurance in the road trial with Hall. They raced over a 7.3 km course and the marathon man beat the miler by thirty seconds.

Being favourite was a new pressure for the Australian. Since his Fukuoka triumph, the sporting public had gradually become aware that Australia had a potential world-beater in an immensely competitive and truly international sport. And like sporting publics everywhere they progressed easily from hopes of success to expectations of success and on to insistence on success. The majority of Australia's armchair athletes weren't interested in PBs or brave second placings. They wanted world records and gold medals — especially gold medals.

The growing awareness of marathon running was illustrated in a humorous way the day before the race. Brisbane's *Daily Sun* published a racecourse-style betting market and potted form on the Games event. The most favoured runners in the *Sun's* market were:

3–1: Rob de Castella, Australia
7–1: Gidamis Shahanga, Tanzania
5–1: Kevin Ryan, New Zealand, and Zacharia Barie, Tanzania
11–2: Juma Ikangaa, Tanzania, Lawrie Whitty, Australia, and John Graham, Scotland

The newspaper's bookie didn't do too badly, although Barie, the 10,000 m silver medallist, eventually scratched from the marathon.

The potted form for some of the top runners also made interesting reading:

'ROB DE CASTELLA (NO. 28) AUSTRALIA.
With a time of 2:08:18 and a great competitive record, he is the man to beat. Under great pressure though.'

'JUMA IKANGAA (623) TANZANIA.
The 20-year-old (more about the ages of Ikangaa later) African champion is claimed by his countrymen to be better than defending Games champion Gidamis Shahanga.'

'MICHAEL GRATTON (233) ENGLAND.
From a country where 20,000 people start in a single marathon. His selectors have judged him one of their best.'

'JOHN GRAHAM (577) SCOTLAND.
De Castella rates him among his strongest rivals, but he has been ill recently.'

'KEVIN RYAN (505) NEW ZEALAND.
A classy international performer slipping into the veteran class, but ran a career best last time out. Dangerous.'

'GIDAMIS SHAHANGA (629) TANZANIA.
The defending champion and superb winner in the 10,000 m on the track last weekend. Will take some beating.'

The marathon suddenly attracted national interest and Rob was a national hero-in-the-making. However, all this added to the pressure, and Gayelene was acutely aware, as she chatted to him on that Thursday evening, of the build-up of tension in her normally easy-going husband.

Mishaps aside, he had prepared himself meticulously. He had freshened up considerably over the ten days before the race, tapering his weekly training from a regular 220 km down to 136 km, reducing his calorific intake accordingly. He had stringently followed a complex carbohydrate-loading routine to maximize the supplies of glycogen stored in his muscle fibres. This was the fuel to carry him through the vital last 10 km of the race he had been building towards, unconsciously and consciously, for fourteen years. Seven days before the start, he sharply decreased the amount of carbohydrate in his diet to trick his body into over-compensating when this type of food became available again and converting more of it than normal into the running fuel, glycogen. On Tuesday morning, three days before the big event, he was still on a low-fat, reduced carbohydrate diet with white meat — fish and chicken — supplying the protein and lots of vegetables making up the bulk. He was confident his slow-twitch muscle fibres had been drained of glycogen by the combination of diet and his daily running routine. To remove the small amount still stored in his fast-twitch fibres and to guarantee the over-compensation response, he did a session of speed work on a track, running six 200 m sprints with 100 m jogs in between.

From midday on Tuesday and throughout Wednesday, he switched to an 80 per cent carbohydrate diet with some white meat to provide protein. He took some trouble to ensure this food was appetisingly presented, in the belief that this would increase the efficiency of his digestive processes. On Thursday, race eve, the carbohydrate content went up to 90 per cent with only a few apricot bars and low-fat cookies to provide lighter relief. He ate boiled whole grain rice, boiled wholemeal noodles and boiled potatoes cooked without their skins because of advice from his father that certain chemicals in the skins could impair digestion. Rob had taken an ample supply of his own noodles to Brisbane and when a Games Village chef began to prepare them, he was soon surrounded by curious and hungry marathon runners. Rob remembered, 'I ended up feeding half the marathon field. I think some of them were afraid not to get stuck into my noodles in case they were the key to some dietary magic formula. The chef was very co-operative in spite of our unusual demands.'

Rob had a mental map of the entire course. He had run over most of it a month before and had driven over its second half five times in the four days before the race, trying to memorize every bend, hill and dip. Different landmarks, checked against split times written on the back of his left hand, would enable him to judge just how far he was from the finish line at the various stages of the race, and how fast he was running. Mentally, he travelled the route again and again. By

8.30 p.m. Gayelene had had enough of the tension and told Rob he should go to bed in anticipation of the morning's early start. He had tried over the previous few nights to wean himself from his usual late retiring hour of 11.30 p.m. He went to bed at 8.45 but, understandably, sleep was elusive. 'I knew what was going to happen the next day,' he said wryly.

At 1.30 a.m., after only three and a half hours sleep, he got up and made himself a few slices of toast and chatted with his room-mate, steeplechaser Peter Larkins.

He went back to bed at 2 a.m. but didn't sleep soundly, dozing off and on. In the wakeful periods he meditated in an effort to relax. At 3.45 a.m. he rose and began to dress. It was pitch black and very quiet.

In the sub-tropical gloom thirty-three other keyed-up marathoners were preparing, like Rob, to push their bodies to the limit in the common quest for glory.

At 4.45, the competitors boarded the bus for the fifteen minute drive to the start-finish in Stanley Street, on the banks of the Brisbane River and across from the darkened towers of the city's business and administrative district. Several of the runners chatted in the dimly lit bus. As one said, 'There's no intense rivalry in a marathon. Everybody in the race knows that everybody else has worked his butt off to get there. No one's egotistical. It's a real leveller.'

Amid the small talk, the Australian was keeping his energies directed, staying on a single mental track.

At 5 a.m. with the sky hinting at dawn, the bus stopped outside the Queensland Surf Life Saving Association offices, 30 m from the start. Rolet de Castella met Rob as he alighted. The elder de Castella was in a tracksuit and obviously excited. Still, he tried to generate calm as he said, 'Good luck, son.'

Rob smiled at the man who had taken him on his first early morning jogs thirteen years earlier. 'Thanks, Dad,' he said. Further on, that other guiding light, Clohessy, was waiting in a press of officials, media people and spectators. The coach had to come to the rescue when a Film Australia crew, part of a big team working on the official film of the Games, zeroed in on his charge. Clohessy explained, 'They wanted to string microphones on Rob and myself and have us go over our race tactics before it was even run. It wasn't the time to be doing that and I had to give them their marching orders.'

The coach and runner walked into the big warehouse that served as the nerve centre for the organization of the race. Clohessy said: 'I chatted with him to see if he had any worries, but he was pretty right. We had had a long session the day before discussing all the aspects of the race so I didn't need to say much. I said ordinary things like, "This is what you've been working for. It's going to be your day. You're definitely ready. I'm sure you're going to run a beauty."'

Rob sat wrapped in a blanket for fifteen minutes, fine-tuning his mental preparation. Then he limbered up with a twenty minute jog through the twilight streets where there were unusual numbers of people about already, moving into position to see the start or to watch the first few kilometres of the racing. The sun was edging up by the time Rob finished his warm-up. It was light enough to see the grandstand erected near the starting line. Its 1,000-seat capacity was already taken up and more people were standing.

'I tried to be very calm. You can't afford to have your pulse rate elevated before a race. You must not have too much adrenalin flowing through the system. You need to save that for the race.'

Rob looked at the other runners shuffling restlessly about. It was hard to decide where the real challenge would be generated. The willowy defending champion, Shahanga, had won the 10,000 m gold medal a week earlier. He was a runner who just could not be dismissed. Three times he had lost contact with the leaders and by all the traditions of distance running, he should have been beaten. Yet each time he fought his way back, finally running away from the field in the final lap. His team-mate, Ikangaa, was highly regarded by the Tanzanians but none of them seemed sure whether he had run 2:12 or 2:21 in winning the All Africa Championship in Cairo earlier in the year. Ikangaa was a tiny man, 154 cm tall, but he moved with relaxed grace as he limbered up. To Rob, he was still just another face in the crowd. The Australian anticipated that the Africans would sit on a runner of his stature. They had not run times to match his and could be expected, like the Ethiopians Balcha and Kedir in successive Stramilano half-marathons, to hang behind while he did the hard work, hoping to grab victory in the last few kilometres by using their superior short-distance speed. A slow race would not be to Rob's advantage so he had a word with the New Zealander, Ryan, another pedigreed road runner with no interest in sprint finishes, and they agreed if the pace was too slow they would run as a team to push it along. Rob explained this allegiance across international boundaries. 'I had known Kevin for years and years and we had raced all over the world together. I understand him and we have a similar approach to tactics. If I had thought one of the other Australians, Lawrie Whitty or Rob Wallace, capable of being up there I might have approached them. But nationalism doesn't matter so much in the marathon. You're not out to psyche your rivals. Everybody is competing against the distance and they all realize that whoever is fittest on the day is going to win.'

So the Australian and New Zealander walked among the crowd of runners — white, black, brown, famous, unknown, aggressive or fearful — to the starting line of an event which would capture the attention and imagination of Australia as no marathon had done in the past.

About 3,000 spectators were close enough to see the smoke from the gun as the field set off. The morning was cool, 14°C, but the humidity was a menacing 94 per cent. There would not be much skin-cooling evaporation in conditions like this and a fast time, theoretically, was not on. The two Tanzanians, accompanied by the Kenyan Sammy Mogare, went straight into the lead. Rob sighed his relief. It would have been terrible to have found himself forced to the front in the first few kilometres of such a long journey because no one else wanted to run fast enough to shake off the sprinters. The Australian settled into a comforting pack of nine runners as they paraded between lines of enthusiasts on the arching Victoria Bridge and almost immediately hit the first of fourteen climbs of more than 5 m that would make the Brisbane marathon a most testing and, ultimately, amazing race.

Free to let themselves go at last, the runners scarcely acknowledged the first incline, dashing up Anne Street between mostly darkened buildings and animated avenues of people. 'Come on, Deek,' came the shouts from the footpaths and the small beer garden at the Crest Hotel. Clohessy had gone to the hotel with the film crew to watch the race on television and he paused outside to give Rob 'a bit of a yell'. Up on the first floor, an eternity from the runners' consciousness, people were starting a champagne breakfast at tables near windows overlooking the road. Gayelene had walked thoughtfully to the hotel from the starting area to have breakfast while she waited for her husband to return at the end of the first stage of the race, a run through the city and out to the airport and back, which would be followed by another return trip, from the city out to Queensland University. She found at the Crest that she was too nervous to eat.

The Africans loped up a 25 m-in-500 m incline and down the other side at a stinging pace. Just after 6.15 Rob reached the first feeding station. Looking up at the digital clock showing elapsed time he was startled to see he had covered the first 5 km in 15 min 09 sec — about two seconds inside a world record schedule. The Africans, running easily, had passed the table without drinking in 14 min 45 sec, snatching a lead of 125 m. It was audacious running, but the Australian, like the other runners and the spectators, thought it would be a short-lived episode.

5 km to 10 km

Rob drank about half of a 300 ml bottle of the glucose-water mixture he had organized for each feeding table. As they ran through the scruffy suburb of Fortitude Valley and out towards the flat road along the river bank, the pack began to close up on the Africans. When Mogare abruptly let go of the Tanzanians' pace and was quickly swallowed up by the field, that seemed a reasonable omen. Rob relaxed and chatted with Ryan. They discussed the surprising number of people who had come out early to cheer them on, the weather, the pace and the tactical possibilities. Talk passed the time and there was not yet a need to concentrate fiercely on the mechanics of running. That would come later with the numbing weariness.

10 km to 15 km

Out past the iron lace grandeur of the Breakfast Creek Hotel and along the flat road through Hamilton and Eagle Farm, the pack led by Rob, Ryan and the Scot, Graham began to catch the Tanzanians. At 10 km the gap was only five seconds, with the leaders having run 5 km in 15:26 and the pack covering the distance in 15:07. There was less apprehension now about the tactical situation. Ryan found the official beverage at the 10 km feeding station a little too strong and threw it away. Rob explained that his drink was a 3 per cent glucose mix and the New Zealander expressed interest. Forbidden by the rules to hand anything to a fellow competitor, the Australian simulated a careless tossing away of his half-full bottle. The New Zealander just failed, amid laughter, to gather the pass.

As they approached the 12.5 km turnaround to begin the run back to the city, the Tanzanians were able to see how much of their lead had been swallowed up. Rob expected them to settle into the pack but instead they 'shot off like a pair of startled rabbits'. They ran the next 5 km in 15:13 while the Australian, leading the pack, clocked 15:23. He was now trailing by fifteen seconds and the Africans were out of sight. This loss of visual contact, which continued for 23 km, imposed a psychological burden on the pursuers which should not be under-estimated. Ron Clarke commented, 'The cool he [de Castella] showed was just fantastic. When the Tanzanians broke away I'd have gone with them. No way in the world would I have stayed back. I would have gone with them and I would have died with them.' Just before the 15 km feeding post, the tousled-headed Sydney runner Lawrie Whitty dropped out with stomach cramps. His best running had been spent in clocking a PB in the wind-swept 10,000 m a week earlier.

15 km to 20 km

Rob grew increasingly uneasy. Indecision, he knew, could be fatal at this stage of the race. He would have to make a choice soon between staying in the security of the pack, where the presence of the others lifts a runner along and makes the distance less tedious, and going out after the Africans before their breakaway developed into a victory lead. Perhaps, as many spectators were beginning to think, it was already too late. He was perspiring freely and feeling clammy in the humidity which had now climbed to saturation point — 100 per cent. Rob carefully wiped himself down at each sponging station and drank at every feeding table. The two leaders were less cautious. Ikangaa, used to the pressure cooker climate of Dar-es-Salaam, drank only twice during the race and Shahanga was only a little more cautious.

The pair — Shahanga a little lop-sided and bent forward, Ikangaa neat, loose and marvellously rhythmical — were widening their lead on the pack, which had been reduced to five runners: de Castella, Ryan, Graham, John Laing of Scotland and the Cypriot Marios Kassianides.

20 km to 25 km

They raced through the Ivory Street Tunnel, usually full of automobile noises and smells, now empty and echoing the slap of their shoes, then back toward the centre of the city where the crowds had thickened noticeably. The leaders, with Shahanga regularly checking his watch, passed the 20 km mark just before 7 a.m. and led by about 180 m.

In Sydney, an 86-year-old nun, a friend of Rob's mother, got up and checked the race on TV. She said a prayer: 'Lift him up, Lord. Take him by the neck, Holy Spirit.' Then she told a friend, 'He'll be all right now.' The Tanzanians sped past the 21.1 km half-marathon mark in 63:40, within a minute of the best achieved on the Australian continent, a 1981 performance by Gerard Barrett who was watching the race as he convalesced from a leg operation. The main difference between the Africans' and Barrett's performance was that the Tanzanians still had another half-marathon to run. They galloped back along Anne Street and past the Crest Hotel and an anxious Gayelene Clews. After they passed she waited nearly a full minute for a glimpse of her husband. 'I thought he had lost it at that stage,' she said. 'They had such a lead . . . all that training. I felt sad for him. No one could pick up so much time and win.'

Clohessy was not so concerned. 'I just thought the Africans were running too fast and were sure to slow up. On the other hand, Rob was running fast enough and he looked really good.' Kassianides, meanwhile, had lost his place among the second division leaders.

25 km to 30 km

The Africans scarcely faltered after their 20–25 km split of 15:11. Rob now had fifty-five seconds to make up after running the split two seconds slower. The Australian realized he could no longer afford to stay with the pack. The leaders weren't coming back to the field as good sense suggested they should. On a hilly course in unfavourable climatic conditions they were still on schedule to run 2:07 and destroy the world record. And they were still out of sight. Rob said, 'I'd tried to pick up the pace to get the pack to come with me. Now I realized I'd have to do it on my own. I didn't know how far they were ahead because I couldn't even see them. Up to this point I'd been running. From here on I really started to compete. I attacked the hills much more aggressively. I always run hills aggressively, because I've trained so much on them and I like conquering them.'

The Tanzanians were, in fact, 300 m in front but their team effort was beginning to come apart with Shahanga conceding a 15 m lead to his compatriot. Rob was now in no-man's-land between the leaders and the pack which was struggling another 130 m back, led by Ryan, the Scots Graham and Laing, and the Englishman Mike Gratton. The string of runners careered along Coronation Drive on the out-and-back leg to Queensland University, past a noisy crowd of about 3,000 on either side of the road at the Regatta Hotel, a popular watering hole for students. Some of them had been up drinking all night in anticipation of the big race and clapped and shouted encouragement but Rob detected disappointment among the clamour. 'I could sense they were resigned to me coming third,' he said. But the Australian was far from beaten. 'I thought I could catch them. I didn't know if I would, but I thought I could.'

30 km to 35 km

He ran strongly along Sir Fred Schonell Drive, attacking the St Lucia hills near the university, but as he turned into the campus to negotiate a flattish 5 km loop there, he was a daunting fifty-eight seconds behind. A fog pall hung over the university, inhibiting the Australian Broadcasting Commission helicopter from adding aerial footage to an otherwise superb coverage of the race. Wreaths of mist lay across the road and the humidity was still only a point or two below saturation. This was the stage when the cold fingers of doubt took hold of Clohessy. 'When Rob didn't appear to be making up any ground and the Tanzanians were still going well, I began to get really worried. The day before, when we had planned the race, Rob said he wanted to make a big effort at about 25 km and I had said, "No, wait. The last 10 km will be the time to pour it on." Now I began to wonder if I hadn't given the wrong advice. For about ten minutes I couldn't get any information on how far he was behind and I was worried all right.'

But Rob stoked up his boilers through the tree-lined university grounds completing the 5 km loop in 15:28. At last he was cutting the Africans' lead back quickly. Although they were still, agonizingly, out of sight, spectators occasionally gave him some indication of the size of the gap. The leaders had slowed and the strain, for the first time, showed on their faces. Shahanga was just hanging on, losing ground on every hill, and Ikangaa's time for the campus loop was twenty seconds slower than the Australian's. Rob thought he finally caught sight of them as he ran out of the university and back on to Sir Fred Schonell Drive. 'They looked so far ahead I thought I was in a different race.' He drove himself at the St Lucia hills which he had always known would be a critical point in the winning or losing of a gold medal. Ikangaa looked over his shoulder.

Abruptly Rob was in trouble. The mildly sick feeling that often accompanies hard running turned suddenly into a knifing pain in the stomach. His stomach muscles began to cramp. 'It was very intense,' he said. 'I had felt some stomach discomfort from the early stages but it became worse when I ran up a very sharp hill along Sir Fred Schonell Drive. I couldn't run easily but I didn't dare slow too much. I had to let go of my bowels and there was some diarrhoea, but it was mostly wind. I ran through the pain which lasted about 700 metres.'

The Tanzanians were clearly in view now and Shahanga was dropping back. Both Africans were struggling on the hills. 'They were running through them rather than over them. I sensed that they must be getting pretty exhausted. But I couldn't be sure.'

After the 32 km mark the TV picture of the African leaders suddenly included a distant figure in green shorts and white singlet. Back at the Crest, Clohessy leapt to his feet as this dramatic moment thrilled millions of Australians and shouted: 'He's closing. He's closing.' A thousand kilometres to the south, distracted commuters brought traffic to a halt on Sydney's Harbour Bridge.

35 km to 40 km

Shahanga, the man who often gave the impression he would run out of his grave to catch an ambitious frontrunner, finally looked really beaten, dropping twenty metres behind Ikangaa. Rob closed the gap on the tiring champion at a charge. It was 100 m, 80, 60, 40, 20. Then on a flat stretch at 37 km he passed the valiant African and the crowds on the footpaths roared and more distant Australians leapt about their lounge rooms like mad people. 'Shahanga didn't have a puff left,' Rob said. 'He didn't have the strength for even a token resistance.'

Ikangaa was now only 80 m ahead. His rhythm was unbroken but his face betrayed the cost of his attempt to write another fabulous chapter in Africa's distance running saga. Almost unknown outside his own land, he had set out to run the greatest marathon in history and now he was paying the price. He looked over his shoulder again at his advancing nemesis.

Near the Regatta Hotel, where many of the fans were close to the end of a different kind of ordeal, Rob pounded up behind the little Tanzanian. The crowd was in uproar and hundreds surged on to the road threatening to impede the runners. At 38 km the Australian moved up to Ikangaa's shoulder and the little man turned toward him, open-mouthed, his face a mixture of surprise, apprehension and defiance. He said later: 'I heard the shouts "Castella, Castella" and I knew the moment had come for him to overcome me.'

The next moment, however, the African surged back sharply to retake the lead.

Such an instant counter-attack would have broken the will of many runners but Rob was not to be denied. He thought, 'Either he's got a lot left or else he's not being very sensible.' Yet he was afraid to ease back in case this allowed the Tanzanian to gather his resources. Once again he drove ahead, looking huge and a little ponderous next to the diminutive African. But Ikangaa put in another spurt and recaptured the lead. So they slugged it out for a kilometre, a desperate riveting duel between two depleted but utterly determined men. Rob took the lead for a third time and was able to pry a little gap.

40 km to Finish

A slight slope slowed the African, but Rob surged powerfully and his lead widened. The previous 5 km had been Ikangaa's slowest split of the race and Rob's fastest: 15:03 for the Australian and a startling tribute to his fitness and strength. 'I was amazed at my time for this 5 km, especially as I had so much pain and couldn't run easily because of the cramp for most of it.'

He didn't know how much of a lead he had built but he was determined to stay ahead of the brilliant little Tanzanian over the final 2,195 metres. He said he experienced a strange blending of strength and exhaustion. 'Although my legs felt weary, I still had my strength left.' He turned into Stanley Street which was now crammed with thousands of people chanting: 'de Castella, de Castella' and relaxed with the awareness of victory. He allowed himself to wave his arms in triumph over the final few metres of the long road, then he bounded across the line in 2:09:18 — 65 seconds slower than Salazar's world best. On the other hand conditions in Brisbane that morning (the 100 per cent humidity had dropped to 88 by race end) made his effort arguably the greatest marathon ever run.

Ikangaa trailed him in by about sixty-five metres to clock 2:09:30, the fastest marathon by an African and an incredible entry to major international competition.

Beyond the finish line there was predictable pandemonium. Gayelene and Clohessy were first to reach the winner. She threw her arms about her sweat bedewed hero and choked out, 'You're beautiful.'

Clohessy grabbed him and hoisted him into the air in mad exuberance. Then the three of them jogged through the roaring, clapping throng as the then Prime Minister of Australia, Malcolm Fraser, joined the photographers falling over each other to get the best angles. Somebody handed Rob a bottle of champagne, which he partly emptied in a sparkling shower over his own head. He had a huge grin and seemed remarkably composed. In the euphoria of victory there was little outward sign of the wear and tear of the contest. He told the journalists crowding about him: 'I thought I was going to blow it, but Pat had told me the race would be decided in the last 10 km. We judged it well . . . it was spot on. I had a stitch and was a little worried with 9 km to go, but I felt strong and knew I could keep going till the finish.'

Clohessy interrupted excitedly, 'What an effort! What a run! It just shows you've got to be patient — that's what won him the race.'

Rob told another questioner, 'I was a little bit concerned when I traded the lead with Ikangaa because every time he passed me he ran strongly. But I gritted my teeth and kept going and I never once looked back. I believe I was running faster today than at Fukuoka (when the stopwatch clicked 60 seconds earlier). I felt stronger and fitter.'

Still with a grin from ear to ear, the Australian went into the Life Saving offices to shower while the rest of the field straggled in. After Ikangaa, the order was: Gratton, England, 2:12:06; Graham, Scotland, 2:13:04; Ryan, New Zealand, 2:13:42; Shahanga, Tanzania, 2:14:25; Laing, Scotland, 2:14:54; Ian Ray, England, 2:15:11; Mike Dyon, Canada, 2:15:22; Wallace, Australia, 2:15:24.

The rest of the long procession ended when Nicholas Akers of the Cayman Islands strode doggedly to the finish, three hours, two minutes and thirty-five seconds after hearing the starter's pistol fire. Six runners, including Whitty, failed to finish.

Adelaide journalist Geoff Roach, covering the race for the Murdoch group of newspapers, heard Rob utter four words in the post-race maelstrom which he thought said it all. The runner told a friend, 'I had no choice.'

Roach wrote: 'No choice but to win. No choice but to summon from every muscle, sinew, tendon and brain cell a supreme, unyielding effort . . . and in the end the most remarkable thing wasn't that the 25-year-old Canberra biophysicist managed to achieve every one of those things and assured forever his place in Commonwealth Games and marathon history. No, the incomprehensible thing was that de Castella looked for all the world as though he could, after a few moments' rest, have gone out and done it all again. He finished composed, coherent and in control of mind and body. After 42.2 km of the most extreme stress and effort, he handed a carnation to his wife Gayelene, kissed and hugged her, consoled a fellow runner who, some thirty minutes after his own finish, was being helped into the medical room, and went on a victory parade. He analysed and recapped every facet of the race for a crushing horde of television, radio and print media interviewers. He even talked eagerly of a possible match race with American Alberto Salazar in Rotterdam next year and conceded, without the slightest trace of over-confidence, that he believed he might eventually run a marathon in 2:07. And then he rode off in the Australian team bus to prepare to receive his gold medal at QE II Stadium in the afternoon.'

After his shower Rob went back outside to the sea of adoring fans and was crowned with a laurel wreath by the Prime Minister's wife, Tamie Fraser, and presented with a trophy. Holding the silver cup aloft he took a victory walk through the crowd. 'I tried to jog but almost fell on my face.'

Ikangaa had a rub-down and then appeared also to be in remarkably good shape. Asked if he was disappointed, the little army lieutenant from Dar-es-Salaam said, 'He's a runner. I'm a runner. We both did our best.'

Ikangaa agreed he had gone out after the world record as well as the gold medal. He commented, 'I was chasing the world's record but it was bad luck for me today. If I had known de Castella's finishing power, I wouldn't have run so slow for the first half of the race.' The other contestants would not find that remark easy to digest.

On the joust for the lead near the Regatta Hotel, the Tanzanian said, 'I sprinted past him because my aim was to check how strong he was. I was impressed with his strength.'

He would also have been impressed with Rob's post-race disclosure that even during that heated struggle he was so in control he didn't once drop into oxygen debt.

Ikangaa concluded, 'I'm now the fastest man in Africa and I was very pleased with my run and also, especially, I was very much pleased with the Australian people cheering for us all the way. For the last three thousand metres I had no strength to run fast again, but I'm not disappointed in losing because I enjoyed the race very much.'

Rob was amazed by the two Tanzanians' lack of interest in the refreshment stations along the route, particularly in view of the humidity. 'I asked one of their coaches why they didn't drink and he said it was better for them to keep running and retain their rhythm. If they stopped to drink they might lose concentration. I couldn't believe it. It's physiological nonsense.'

The Africans' lack of inhibition is often and convincingly cited as a reason for their successes over the long distances, but the Australian feels they lose more than they gain by not adhering to conventional wisdom. He remarked, 'I think they are greatly hampered by their attitude. Look at Ikangaa's statement that he would have run faster in the early stages if he had known what a strong finisher I was. If he had gone any faster he would just have died earlier. I would have caught him at an earlier stage of the race, that's all.'

The Tanzanians decided to attack the world record after driving over the course in a bus and judging it to be suitable for a fast time. Rob said, 'If they think that course is fast, they must have some real beauties at home!'

Ikangaa displayed the remarkable ageing properties that are becoming characteristic of African runners. He told the press conference he was eighteen, but added a year when chatting with Rob a few minutes later. Melbourne journalist Geoff Slattery did some sleuthing among the Tanzanians and declared Ikangaa was really twenty-three. There have been suggestions that many Africans are less than frank about their ages because they anticipate scholarships at US universities where age limits can trim their track careers and so curtail their academic pursuits. But there is also a strong cultural factor. In rural Africa, ages are not considered important and birthdays are not celebrated. Many runners would not have given a thought to the year, let alone date, of their births until they entered international competition and were confronted with their first Western-style entry forms. Their response to the question of age can only be described as flexible.

The times clocked by Ikangaa and de Castella confounded the Brisbane running community. Local athletes had calculated that a 2:10 clocking would be at least the equal of Salazar's 2:08:13 world best. So, by their reckoning Rob had run the equivalent — in favourable conditions — of a 2:07:31 marathon, or better. Clarke, who watched the TV coverage, said, 'It has to be the best marathon ever run. I've seen the course and have spoken to people who have raced over it and we all considered that a time of 2:10 or even 2:11 would be equal to a world record. Rob clocked 2:09 on that course which would have to be worth 2:07 on any other course. With all those hills it's the toughest course I've seen. I'd love to see him race against Salazar and the other top Americans. I know who I'd back.'

Clohessy was a little more cautious. 'It's hard to compare performances under different conditions. There are so many factors. It's guess work really. And you shouldn't overlook a very positive aspect of this race — the competitive situation. But if you had a similar contest, without the humidity and the hills on, say, a fast point-to-point course with a bit of a following wind, then even being extremely conservative, it would have to be inside 2:08, wouldn't it?'

When those comments were added to Rob's assertion, 'I could have run a faster time. But I wasn't out to run a fast time. I was out to win the gold medal', and his obviously excellent immediate post-race physical state, exciting prospects opened for the future. The patient years invested in gradually adapting the young runner's body to accept the rigours of running at world-record levels had paid their first golden dividend. His Commonwealth Games victory left the impression that, although he might never run a 2:06:30 marathon, he would if he had to — if, once again, he was left with no choice.

For the moment, those who had followed his career were satisfied to have witnessed one of history's greatest marathon contests and to accept Geoff Roach's urging to mark down 8 October 1982, as 'the Day of Deek'.

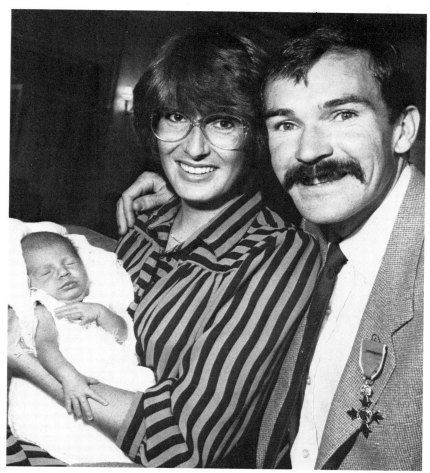

Two-week-old Krista was totally relaxed at her first vice-regal appointment, Dad's investiture as a Member of the British Empire at Government House, Canberra, on 13 October 1983.

The scene of the greatest challenge: during a 1983 visit to Los Angeles Rob inspected the marathon course and the Olympic stadium where the race will finish.

CHAPTER FOURTEEN

Physical Frontiers

The Fukuoka success changed Rob's life, but its shock waves were ripples compared with those that engulfed him after his Brisbane triumph. He was now a true national hero, Australia's first publicly acclaimed marathon celebrity, and honours were heaped upon him. At a gala evening in Melbourne he was named Australia's Sportsman of the Year and took home a second ornate trophy for producing the Performance of the Year. At another glamorous dinner, in Sydney, he was named the Australian Broadcasting Commission's top sportsman for 1982 and at year's end he was declared a Member of the British Empire in the Queen's New Year's Honours List.

The presentations and less formal personal congratulations came in an uninterrupted stream but some of the most satisfying were at the finish of the Big M Marathon in Melbourne when American Bill Rodgers rode a tailwind to a 2:11:08. He was followed by a procession of Australians in personal best times, including Grenville Wood, second in 2:12:50, and Jeff Coole, third in 2:13:57. Rob recalled, 'I went to the Big M as a TV commentator for Channel 7 and handed out a few of the medals. People I didn't know came up to me and thanked me for the motivation I had given them through the Brisbane Commonwealth Games race. I hope that had something to do with the fast times, although I think the wind was quite a factor.'

He was critical of the organization of the event which had more of the informality of a fun run than the professionalism of a big marathon. 'A marathon shouldn't be treated like that. It's a major effort. People get themselves up psychologically to compete and if it doesn't go smoothly it can be a big disappointment. They can lose interest and miss out on a lot of future satisfaction from the sport.'

There was no danger of Rob losing interest. Asked if he felt a little let down after achieving a major ambition in Brisbane, he laughed. 'Not at all. A good performance always motivates me. Now I'm ready for the next 50,000 km of training.'

Some of his career's most important facts and figures emerged from medical examination rooms, the laboratory at the Institute of Sport and from his training log as he monitored his recovery from the Commonwealth Games race.

As expected, his pulse rate was elevated and he felt lethargic for the first few weeks. He suffered mild headaches but the symptoms of damage disappeared much more quickly than they had after Fukuoka. Rob said, 'Recovery was much quicker and smoother, partly because I had another year of quality training under my belt and also, I think, because the Fukuoka run itself must have had a toughening effect. It did a lot for me, both physically and mentally. Also, after Fukuoka I felt under more pressure. I was trying to come up for the Australian track season which was in full swing. This time there was not so much urgency. I was able to relax with some easy jogging at distances between 5 km and 13 km in the first week and I totalled only 61 km.'

His training log showed the speed of his recovery after that 61 km week. In the next seven days he ran 122 km, in the third week 146 km and from there on it was back over 160 km.

Dick Telford, the physiologist at the institute, believed Rob recovered quickly because he was not fully extended in Brisbane. Telford said, 'He could have run faster and I estimate that he finished at about 85 per cent of his capacity. He ran so strongly over the last 8 km that he clearly had a lot in reserve.'

Pat Clohessy also believed there was room for improvement. After spending a few weeks digesting the ramifications of the Brisbane race, he said he believed Rob would continue to improve for another three or four years and would eventually run inside 2:07. 'I think he will hit his peak at the Los Angeles Olympics and beyond. He is still making progress and can improve in certain areas. His speed, his balance and his efficiency can all be improved.'

Rob commented, 'To get under 2:07 I would have to run on a fast, flat course and probably with a pacemaker. But I think I can achieve it. I'm still improving. I ran a very conservative race in Brisbane. I held myself back and I was able to finish very strongly. I like to finish strongly. I think that psychologically and physiologically it is best to run like this, rather than tire badly and really have to push yourself beyond the point of exhaustion. I don't know whether I have good times because I am stronger and fitter or because I don't push myself as hard as people like Salazar.'

A runner has to live on the physical frontiers to achieve times like 2:09:18 on a hilly course in high humidity. Rob suffered damage in the race which provided sports scientists and doctors in Canberra and Melbourne with material for original research. His legs had collided with the Brisbane tarmac about 42,000 times during the run and his style is not light and floating. He explained, 'All the pounding diverts blood to the legs and this has several effects. One is that blood is drained away from the bowels and the lining of the stomach and the tissue dies off. All this is going on deep inside your body and it's hard for the specialists to be sure exactly what is taking place. They can't do the sort of on-the-spot investigations that would give them a solid diagnosis.'

The effect, as far as a runner's feelings are concerned, is pain and, sometimes, stomach cramps. After the race dead tissue peels away from the stomach lining, causing more pain and diarrhoea — probably the kind of black diarrhoea that so worried Derek Clayton after Antwerp. Sometimes Rob gets 'pretty bad diarrhoea' after a race and can't eat or drink for four or five hours. The faster tempo road races — between 10 km and 25 km — when the pounding is more severe than in a marathon, are the worst. Few runners complain of suffering in the same way, probably because they don't run as hard as Rob or Clayton.

Rob revealed that a Canberra specialist was studying the problem. 'He's doing a bit of library research. Superficially, the peeling away of the stomach lining is not terribly different from a woman's menstruation. I don't think it is serious because the tissue regenerates. The doctors have given me some tablets, muscle relaxants and things like that, to take after a race and they seem to help. Long, fast road runs must be one of the most stressful activities I know. Cyclists and swimmers are cushioned from the kind of jarring that long-distance runners suffer through their bodies. Really, we don't know how much damage is done to the body in a fast marathon because hardly any research at all has been done on elite runners. I think we are breaking new frontiers with human performance in seeing what our bodies can achieve and what they can absorb.'

Laboratory tests showed another alarming symptom of the race's after-effects. Rob's blood was found to contain high levels of the enzyme Creatine Phosphate Kinase (CPK) which is known to flood the bloodstreams of victims of severe heart attacks. Naturally, there were thoughts of Rolet de Castella's possibly genetic heart problem, but medical science could offer a reassuring answer this time. The CPK enzymes were a by-product of muscle damage. In a coronary case, the damaged muscle is the heart but in a runner's case the enzymes are almost certainly released into the system by trauma to the leg muscles. Investigations into Rob's CPK levels could eventually have an unwelcome spin-off for some of the young swimmers training five hours a day at the Institute of Sport.

Rob said: 'Swimmers are often driven very hard by their coaches and I find the amount of work they do, churning up and down the pool, a motivating factor when I get discontented with my own lot. But they are human and they sometimes feign injury or illness to get some respite from training routines. In the laboratory we're working on ways to use the CPK count to determine the severity of a muscle injury and also as a gauge to an athlete's condition. So a totally depleted runner or swimmer could be told to take a lay-off before doing himself damage. If a swimmer claims he is totally spent, it might be possible to check his CPK count and, if necessary, order him back into the pool. It will be terrible for malingerers.'

Rob laughed, but not without compassion. He understood the lot of the five-hours-a-day swim kids.

He and Clohessy made some fine adjustments to his training routine. There would now be a gym session five days a week at lunch times, split between power-producing circuit exercises and injury-preventing stretching. Whenever possible, the runner would fit in an afternoon nap between work and his evening training session. He had been tired before the Brisbane race and before some of his overseas runs because he had tried to fit too many activities into his routine. He recognized the fact. 'I was trying to do too much: work, my training, and other engagements as well. I'll take things much more easily before my big races in the future.'

Another improvement in Rob's 'total environment' came when Clohessy accepted a coaching job at the Institute of Sport. Their relationship had continued under the tyranny of distance after the runner's move to Canberra in 1981, but now they would be colleagues on the Institute's staff and neighbours in Australia's biggest country town. Clohessy's appointment had to have the personal approval of the then Prime Minister, Malcolm Fraser, and the coach took extended leave from Xavier College to take up the post early in 1983. The Institute's administrator, Peter Bowman, expressed the general delight. 'We're tickled pink to be getting Pat. His results speak for themselves and we feel his presence will attract runners who might otherwise not have applied for scholarships.'

Clohessy too was pleased. 'There hasn't been a fulltime distance coach at the Institute and I'm excited by the challenge. It will make my relationship with Rob so much easier and, hopefully, there will be some promising young runners joining the Institute when the applications for scholarships are worked out.'

Among those accepted to train under Clohessy's guidance were John Andrews, Steve Austin, Steve Foley, the talented Victorian middle-distance man Pat Scammell and Rob's brother Nick de Castella.

As he waited for the appointment to be approved, Clohessy mused about the future of his partnership with Rob. 'The Commonwealth Games race has made a lot of people sit up and take notice. It has placed Rob in a different situation. Young people mature and look for their own directions in life. My coaching has always been aimed at making the runners self-sufficient, encouraging them to make their own decisions but also assuring them they have somebody there to back them up and help them through the difficult patches. If he now decides to make a shift, to go out on his own, I won't be disappointed. I'll have the satisfaction of knowing we have shown it can be done. We've proved that our system works. A young Australian who is patient and dedicated and uses his good sense and our accumulated experience can become the best in the world.'

Such a shift was the furthest thing from Rob's mind. In fact, he relished having his friend and adviser in Canberra to watch his progress and help plan his timetables for training and competition.

Two months after the Games, Rob went to New Zealand to take part in a series of road races featuring the Kiwi national heroes John Walker, Rod Dixon and Dick Quax as well as the great Norwegian Grete Waitz. Rob is normally a tranquil soul, not given to paranoia, but he found it hard in New Zealand to shake off the feeling he was being followed.

Quax took a marathon in moderate time and Dixon an 8 km road race in Wellington to set the scene for the Australian's first appearance, a 12 km contest around the hilly streets of inner Auckland. Dixon, the Olympic 1,500 m bronze medallist in 1972 and fourth placer in the Olympic 5,000 m in 1976, was in superb form. He had been living and racing in the United States where he was seldom beaten over 10–15 km distances and had run an impressive debut marathon in 2:11:21 early in 1982. After that the confident Kiwi was asked about his potential in the long run and said he would clock 2:07:38 some day. Then he added as an afterthought, 'Eventually, I will run a 2:05. Of course, by then somebody may be running 2:03.'

In the Auckland race, the vastly experienced 32-year-old ran shoulder-to-shoulder with Rob until they swung into a final stretch where they had to push directly into a strong breeze. The lanky New Zealander then shifted behind the Australian, using his body as a windshield. Try as he might, Rob could not shake him off. Dixon unwound his venomous kick in the last few metres to win by two seconds in 34:17. American Tom Wysoki was third and the great miler, John Walker, struggled home fourth more than ninety seconds behind the winner. Waitz showed her style in finishing fifteenth overall in 38:32 and well ahead of a strong field of New Zealand women.

Rob was delighted to be so competitive in his first race back. 'I felt a lot better than I did after Fukuoka when it took me several races to get back into form. Last year I just didn't have a chance to settle down. This time it was a lot quieter and my recovery was better.'

But what could he do to beat the speed that had enabled Dixon to run 3:33:9 for 1,500 m? Their next race was around the flatter streets of Christchurch in the South Island and the 15 km distance was more to the Australian's liking. In a classic duel between speed and strength, Rob's only option was to push the pace as hard as he could and once again he demonstrated his remarkable freedom from stopwatch inhibitions. He tore off at the start with Dixon and Wysoki at his back and careered past the first 5 km marker at close to fourteen minutes. He said, 'Wysoki was with us initially but he just exploded at about 4 km. Then it was Dixon and me and I was going flat out. There was no question of surging. I was just flat to the boards.'

Hard as Rob went, he couldn't shake his Kiwi shadow. They rocketed past the 10 km point in 28:10, six seconds faster than the Australian's track PB for the distance. Then they actually accelerated! Even so, the New Zealander, running with graceful rhythm, held on and used his sprint over the final 200 m to win by four seconds in a stunning 41:30, 1:39 faster than Kenyan Mike Musyoki's unofficial road world record of 43:09.

A simple mathematical exercise showed they had run the third 5 km in 13:20 — an impossibly fast split. A remeasure of the course was ordered and it was found to be about 400 m short. Rob commented, 'We would have beaten the world record anyway and the time converts to a better one than Musyoki's. But as far as the statisticians are concerned all that effort was for nothing.'

The race was strikingly similar to the 1981 Stramilano when Rob's uninhibited front-running set up another world record, which he lost in the sprint for home. Frustratingly, he was now the world's second-fastest in history over 15 km (adjusting the Christchurch time from 14.6 km) the half-marathon, 25 km and the marathon. Typically, he laughed about his situation. 'I'll get up there one of these days,' he said.

Dixon confessed that he had been in deep trouble in the first half of the race and only settled happily into stride later on. Rob reflected, 'What I should have done to stop him getting into his rhythm was to have slowed it down almost to a stop a couple of times and then shot off again. You live and learn.'

In spite of the defeat, the race showed Rob to be near his best and he approached his next event, the annual Emil Zatopek 10,000 m track run in Melbourne, with the intention of improving his PB of 28:16:12 set in 1980. It was a long way from the 27:25:61 best of his main marathon rival, Alberto Salazar, and he and Clohessy were convinced he could run a lot faster. Before the race it appeared that the main problem in achieving a good time would be lack of competitive stimulus. This turned out to be anything but accurate. The little, wavy-haired Sydney runner, John Andrews, 24, who had benefited from Clohessy's conditioning advice and the experience of a seventh placing in the Commonwealth Games 5,000 m, ran with Rob all the way and despite his reputation as a sit-and-wait tactician, forged to the lead four times before being repassed. His fifth attack, 180 m from home, was decisive. Rob could not match his sprint for the tape and Andrews' 59 sec. last lap gave him victory in 28:09:7, thirty-one seconds faster than his previous best. He said: 'I'd hoped for a good time, but not that good. Had I been that sharp at the Commonwealth Games it's pretty fair to say I would have got a medal.'

Rob's time was a PB 28:12:2, but he was left shaking his head in frustration. 'I just don't seem able to move my legs fast enough in track races. I felt strong, but I just didn't have enough leg speed.'

Andrews also won their next track contest, a Melbourne 5,000 m, and in late January the Sydney town planner confirmed his improvement when he raced on short, twinkling legs ahead of the field in the Australian cross-country trial race in Sydney's Centennial Park. It was a scorching day and while his rivals drooped, Andrews bolted away from them up a series of steep climbs to win unchallenged by 200 m. Nick de Castella, 22, stole some of the limelight when he collapsed across the line in third place, flattened by heat exhaustion. Rob spent some time the next day searching Canberra supermarkets for newspapers with photographs of his brother's swallow dive. Rob had missed the trial because he was still recovering from a bout of food poisoning.

Nick's game run earned him a place in the national team for the World Cross-country at Gateshead, England, in March. Rob was included along with other non-trialists Lawrie Whitty and Rob McDonald. It was Nick's first international selection. The team was: Rob de Castella, John Andrews, Max Little, Nick de Castella, Whitty, McDonald, Bryan Lewry and Adam Hoyle.

CHAPTER FIFTEEN

Operation Alberto

Rob had scarcely crossed the finishing line in Brisbane before talk began of a match race with Alberto Salazar. The inaugural Track and Field World Championships in Helsinki, Finland, in August 1983 seemed the logical venue, but Salazar was refused an exemption from the US selection race for the event and promptly announced he would only contest the 10,000 m. The Cuban-born American's career had always wavered between the road and the track and although he had achieved instant success in US marathons, he often hinted that his heart was really in track running. Like Rob he was frequently beaten in shorter races by runners with faster sprints but he had run 13:11:93 for 5,000 m and 27:25:61 for 10,000 m. In 1982 the authoritative *Track & Field News* magazine ranked him second in the world in the longer event. Salazar said he would rather win the Olympic 10,000 m than the marathon if he was given a clear choice, because there were better runners in the track race. He said, 'I'll probably never have the superiority in the 10,000 that I now enjoy in the marathon but I believe I can be the world record holder in the 10. If I have run a 27:10 before the Games and no one else has been under 27:22, then I'll run the 10,000 and the marathon. If a whole group of us are together in terms of time I'll probably just run the marathon.'

Rob, who allowed himself no such distractions from the marathon, said shortly after the Brisbane race, 'I want to run against Salazar just to sort out once and for all which of us is the best. From what I've heard, Salazar says he doesn't expect to race against me until the Olympics. It's disappointing for me, but I suppose he's got more to lose by entering a race against me.'

The fact that both runners were managed by the same company, International Management Group of America (IMG) added a novel twist to the international manoeuverings aimed at getting them to the same starting line. IMG, naturally, wanted to see them race only when the financial stakes were as high as possible and preferably when sponsorship deals could be linked to international coverage by satellite-relayed TV. Two European races on fast courses, Rotterdam and Antwerp, were scheduled for April–May, the most suitable period for both runners, giving them time to recover for their respective events in Helsinki in August. Rob was keen but Salazar, initially, was not.

In late November 1982, the focus of negotiations swung back to Australia where the local arm of Rupert Murdoch's international media organization, News Ltd, announced it would provide $1 million to sponsor an Australian Marathon to be run in Sydney each June for three years. The intention was laudable. By agreement with the Athletic Union of Australia, the race would combine the annual national championship with a mass participation event in the style of the London and New York marathons and would offer $28,000 in cash and about the same amount in other prizes to the winners and place-getters in various categories. The money would be held in trust by the AAU so no rules of amateurism would be infringed. The event would be covered live by Murdoch's Sydney TV station, Channel 10.

Announcing the race in the *Australian,* John Hoggett wrote: 'Negotiations are underway to have Commonwealth Games marathon champion Rob de Castella compete. His superb performance in Brisbane saw the event come of age as a spectator sport in this country. De Castella, who only runs one or two marathons a year, has not yet drawn up his programme for next season, but he has agreed to act as technical adviser for the event... World record-holder Alberto Salazar is unlikely to compete. Salazar is now a member of Mark McCormack's sporting stable and the asking price, just to get him to the starting line, is believed to be around the six-figure mark.'

However, timing, rather than cash, eventually ruled the big two out. June's milder temperatures made it a good month to run in

Sydney where heat and humidity are against fast marathon times during more than half the year, but June would obviously clash with the World Championships in August 1983. It also would be too close to the Los Angeles Games in 1984 for Olympic runners to commit themselves. So it seemed the Australian Marathon was unlikely to attract the very best athletes before June 1985, at the earliest. On the other hand its success as a people's event was assured when the Wang computer company joined News Ltd as a major sponsor and sparkling times were recorded all through the field in its initial running.

Meanwhile, a group of Queensland businessmen, inspired by the Commonwealth Games, wanted to stage a major marathon in their State. They took a different tack. When and under what conditions, they asked IMG, would the two runners be available to contest a race along a point-to-point course on the garish Gold Coast holiday strip? The businessmen had an informal agreement with the Queensland athletic authorities to reschedule the established Gold Coast Marathon and shape it around a meeting between the two fastest marathoners in the world.

During Christmas week the announcement came. The race would go ahead on 1 May with a TV audience of 200 million. It would be run early in the morning to avoid Queensland's lingering autumn heat and to enable peak-viewing-time audiences in the US to watch it live. There would be prize money of $100,000, plus a $50,000 bonus to the winner if the world record fell. The field would be limited to twenty or twenty-five runners with an entry standard of 2:12. It was hoped that Japan's Toshihiko Seko and Tanzania's Juma Ikangaa would be among the acceptors but only one other Australian, Grenville Wood, was likely to get a start.

When Rob expressed enthusiasm for the idea, he was criticized for passing up the Australian Marathon where the money was less attractive. He responded calmly. 'The money obviously is of importance and you have to be professional in your outlook. However, the criterion I use in determining my programme is what is best for my athletic career, not my bank balance. The marathon in Sydney is too close to the World Championships and I want to run against Salazar.'

The American also professed to be swayed by the challenge rather than the dollars. 'I'll run in Australia instead of at Boston,' he said.

'De Castella and Seko are both supposed to be there. I'll go there because I have always had the desire to compete against the best.'

This was Salazar the self-conscious Latin American talking. In 1980 he told an interviewer why *machismo*, the testing of one's manhood, mattered to him. 'It's a way of living to us. It's to be emotional, to be courageous, to have some guts. I'm not part of the Anglo-Saxon tradition and I think I treat running differently ... To me, what's important is the challenge of seeing who's better, of proving myself. It's not just catching another runner at the tape, but taking him to a point where he has to say "To hell with it" and gives up. I like the marathon because it's one race where you can find out who's really the toughest.'

There was no doubt about Salazar's toughness. Training mates at Oregon University in Eugene had nicknamed him 'the mule' because of his stubborn refusal to be beaten. At Falmouth in 1978 he ran himself close to death to win a 10 km road race in a heatwave. He collapsed and was packed in ice to bring down his temperature. So severe was his condition that he was given the last rites of the Catholic Church. Two years later, at the age of 22, he declared he would run inside 2:10 in his first marathon and ran 2:09:41 to win the 1980 New York event. A year later he boasted he would break the world record in New York. (His coach Bill Dellinger confessed, 'Alberto is modest but he is also honest and sometimes his honesty walks all over his modesty.') He ran 2:08:13 to beat Clayton's mark. In 1982 he won an exciting duel with Dick Beardsley at Boston — 2:08:51 to 2:08:53 — and then spent nearly fifty minutes on his back being fed intravenous fluids, with his body temperature having gone haywire and dropping as low as 29° C, compared with a normal 37 degrees. He had run four marathons, winning them all and had always clocked inside 2:10.

Alberto Salazar would not be beaten easily and his approach made it seem unlikely the world record would survive his meeting with Rob. 'The marathon is like a bullfight,' he told American writer Eric Olsen. 'There are two ways to kill a bull, for instance. There's the easy way, for one. But all the great matadors end up dead or mauled because for them killing the bull is not nearly as important as how they kill the bull. They always approach the bull at greatest risk to themselves, and I admire that. In the marathon, likewise, there are two ways to win. There's the easy way if all you care about is winning. You hang back and risk nothing, then kick and try to nip the leaders at the end. Or you can push, challenge the others, make it an exciting race, risking everything. Maybe you lose, but as for me, I'd rather run a gutsy race, pushing all the way and lose, than run a conservative, easy race only for a win.'

Rob paid tribute to 'the mule'. 'I know he is a great runner and very gutsy. I'm sure if the conditions are good when we meet the world record will go. I think we are both capable of running under 2:08. He would probably have me pegged over a short distance, but I'm confident I can beat him in a marathon.'

Pressed about a possible time resulting from their confrontation, Rob replied, 'I'm certainly not placing any limitations on myself.'

The Australian's hopes that the race would be in Queensland and therefore a possible source of inspiration to his young countrymen began to crumble when the International Amateur Athletic Federation (IAAF) intervened. Since the liberalizing of its amateurism rules and the legalizing of prize money, the IAAF had been watching developments on the international road racing scene with obvious unease. The controlling body was particularly wary about losing its monopoly on the staging of meetings and the resultant flow of sponsorship and TV funds. It had a rule barring meetings or races organized by runners themselves or their agents and invoked it to stop the Gold Coast event, which it apparently regarded as the creation of IMG. The IAAF sent a telex to the AAU instructing it to refuse to sanction the race.

When an alternative was proposed in New Zealand, the IAAF used the same procedure to make sure it was stillborn.

So IMG and the two runners, both now committed mentally to a meeting in April–May, looked for a race already approved by the IAAF. A quick check on the possibilities identified the third annual Rotterdam Marathon in Holland on 10 April as the best venue for the world heavyweight championship of road running. It was on a fast, flat course, usually run in ideal weather and already had a top-class field. The Mexicans, Rodolfo Gomez and Jose Gomez, were taking altitude training to the pinnacle by preparing in La Paz, Bolivia, at more than 4,000 m above sea level. It is difficult for visitors from lower regions to stroll around La Paz without discomfort, yet the unrelated Gomezes were pursuing their normal training routine in the oxygen-thin air of the world's highest capital. If their experiment worked, it would revolutionize distance running. Already Rodolfo was talking in terms of a 2:07 marathon. Holland's Olympic silver medallist, European champion and European record-holder, Gerard Nijboer, was ready to take on the Mexicans but he had been overshadowed at home recently by a new whiz kid, Cor Lambregts, who was said to have run a half-marathon in close to an hour. Armand Parmentier, an improving Belgian, would be crossing the border and Portugal's Carlos Lopes, a brilliant track and cross-country performer, would be trying to complete a marathon for the first time after dropping out of two New York races.

The Rotterdam officials could scarcely believe their good fortune when the two fastest marathoners in the world agreed to join their already impressive line-up. But they pointed out that big financial stakes were not possible because they had exhausted their race budget attracting the runners already entered. It didn't matter. Money was now secondary to the contest and Rob and Alberto were committed to meet on the three-lap course around a park in the suburbs of the world's biggest port. Negotiations began for Dutch television to transmit the live action around the world.

There was some lingering uncertainty while the two runners' national controlling bodies fumbled their ways towards giving them approval to compete, but even before the last of the red tape was untangled Rob decided to invite his brother-in-law, Graham Clews, to make the trip to Europe with him as his training partner. Clews had been on the fringes of national selection for several seasons, finishing eighth in the World Cross-country selection trial. The trip would be like the realization of a dream for him and Rob got so much pleasure from anticipating the thrill the offer would give Clews, he dragged out breaking the news to him.

Before leaving on the latest of his whirlwind racing tours to the US, Rob took Clews aside at Canberra airport and told him gravely, 'I've got something important to tell you when we get home.'

Clews replied, 'What is it about?'

'Leave it until I get home,' said Rob, mysteriously.

Clews worried throughout the farewells and during the drive home. He said later, 'The worst thing I could think of was that Robert and Gayelene had decided to leave Canberra and spend a full year in the US leading up to the Los Angeles Olympics.'

Meanwhile, Rob jetted from a searing Australian summer, with bushfires blazing along the southern rim of the continent, to snowbound Ireland where he virtually tumbled from the plane into an international cross-country race. His fourth placing was something of a minor miracle in the circumstances and soon afterwards he was back in the skyways, winging toward sunny Florida and the Gasparilla 15 km road race. Thrusting jet lag and stopwatch inhibitions aside, the Australian charged straight into the lead and pounded out the first 10 km in 28:06 (faster than his recent track PB) and finished in 42:46, an arresting twenty-two seconds inside the previous world best. American Greg Meyer, who set a US record in second place, commented, 'What de Castella did was amazing. He came here on a legitimate course that has been tested through the years by some of the best, and he simply embarrassed the world record. He is as tough as a bull.'

Rob said, 'I felt so good and comfortable the whole way, the fast pace never crossed my mind. After about seven miles [11 km] I knew I was okay and just tried to enjoy the race. It's really nice to get a world's best at last after being number two so often.'

The performance comprehensively wiped out the frustration of the short-course 'record' in Christchurch and gave Rob a good deal of motivation at a handy time in relation to his coming marathon. It also earned him $7,000: $5,000 for first place and a $2,000 bonus for the world best time, all paid into his AAU-administered trust fund in Australia.

The next engagement was to be a preliminary skirmish against Salazar over 5,000 m on the boards at New York's Madison Square Garden, but the Big Apple was frosted by blizzards on the night and the meeting was cancelled. Rob was determined to keep up his mileage, despite the weather. He put on a track suit, a skivvy and a quilted jacket and ran 30 km around Central Park where the weather had at least cleared away all the muggers.

A win at 10 km wrapped up his tour and Rob returned to Australia, and an anxious Graham Clews.

On the drive home from the airport Clews asked, 'By the way, what is the bad news?'

Rob replied, 'I want to ask you a really big favour. But it means you can't run in the national titles.'

'Anything to help,' said Clews, with a sinking heart. 'It doesn't matter. What is it?'

'I'll tell you when we get home.'

When they finally settled in the sitting room, Rob, struggling to suppress his grin, said, 'It's like this. I've decided to run the marathon in Rotterdam and I need a training partner. I want you to come with me.'

Clews looked over at Gayelene and burst out, 'He's not serious, is he?'

Rob laughed, 'It means you'll miss the national titles and the Nike Marathon in Canberra . . .'

Clews, beginning to dance, shouted, 'He is serious, isn't he!'

CHAPTER SIXTEEN

Rotterdam

Conditions were ideal just before the start of the Rotterdam Marathon with the temperature edging above 10°C and sunlight brightening the streets, quays and canals of the great port. There had been a week of talk about a world record and an old warrior, Chris Brasher, looked distracted as he strolled through the excited crowd at the start–finish. Asked by a stranger how he thought the race would go, the 1956 Olympic steeplechase champion replied, 'You realize, one of these splendid young men, Salazar or de Castella, will be left with his life in ruins within little more than two hours?'

The splendid young men arrived by different routes to adjoining rooms in a little country hotel in Holland after having a preliminary skirmish at the World Cross-country Championships in Gateshead, England. Salazar had suffered a groin injury in the US cross-country trial but this hadn't stopped him publicly stating his intention of winning at Gateshead. Rob, who wasn't quite so overtly ambitious, had an interesting demonstration of the mind's role in athletics when he watched Graham Clews compete in a local event on the day before his own race. The tall, bearded Australian led the field up a long, muddy climb in the later stages and looked set for a comfortable victory when he suddenly faltered. Clews ruefully recalled, 'I was running pretty strongly ahead of. a bunch of anonymous, rather weedy looking Englishmen when I heard spectators shouting, "Come on Hughie Jones, come on Dave Cannon." I thought to myself, what am I doing leading celebrities like them? That doubt cost me the race. It was a good lesson.'

The Gateshead world title race was over six twisting, hilly 2,000 m laps and began sensationally when Miruts Yifter chose the wrong time to pose for a photographer and missed the start and Mohammed Kedir lost a shoe. However, another Ethiopian, Bekele Debele, who had been running competitively for only eighteen months, was ready to fill the breach. He covered the leaders until halfway, then tried to get away before thinking better of it and dropping back into the pack. The leading group had been whittled to eight by the second-last lap when Rob launched a long drive for home. He dislodged two of his rivals but Debele, Salazar, Carlos Lopes, Antonio Preito of Spain and Some Muge of Kenya refused to be shaken. With 800 m left, Debele passed the Australian whose lack of sharp preparation had caught up with him, and only Lopes, Muge and Salazar were able to match the green-vested Ethiopian's acceleration. In the final 400 m, Salazar fell back a little and the other three got up on their toes and sprinted for the tape in the closest finish in the event's eighty-year history. Debele won in 36:52 and the other results were: Lopes 36:52; Muge 36:52; Salazar 36:53; Preito 36:56, and de Castella 37:00. This matched Rob's previous highest placing in the event and he led the Australians to their best team placing, fourth behind Ethiopia, the US and Kenya. The other Australian results were: 21 John Andrews 37:36; 34 Lawrie Whitty 37:52; 39 Bryan Lewry 38:03; 45 Rob McDonald 38:10; 48 Max Little 38:12; 81 Adam Hoyle 30:49 and 109 Nick de Castella 39:20. There were 210 finishers representing twenty-four national teams.

Salazar flew home for the final weeks of his marathon preparation while Rob and the rest of the Australians travelled to Milan for yet another tilt at the Cinque Mulini. Sharpened by his Gateshead run, Rob took control of the race in the second of four laps and delighted his Milanese friends and supporters by decisively beating local hero Alberto Cova and the two very fast East German track men, Werner Schildhauer and Hans-Jorge Kunze. Rob said, 'It was just great to win after all the years of trying; a really good one to notch up. Our Italian friends were really excited. I was a bit worried because my back had been a bit troublesome at home and there is a lot of sharp turning and ducking under doorways, but it came through well.'

Rob recovered quickly from the testing race and two days later had a solid two-and-a-half hour hit-out in the forest near Berg-en-

Dal in eastern Holland, where the Rotterdam organizers had hidden him away from pre-race pressures. World one-hour track record-holder Jos Hermens followed Rob on a bicycle and was still shaking his head days later and muttering, 'So strong, so strong.'

The Australian felt in better shape than he had been before the Commonwealth Games and thought only Holland's prevailing cold, blustery weather could prevent a world record. He said, 'Media commitments helped tire me out a bit before the Commonwealth Games and my back was worrying me. The organizers here have been very understanding and have made it easy for me to settle in. They have booked me under the name of Mr Roberts and the distance from Rotterdam is great enough to deter most curious media people. There are miles of beautiful forests stretching across the German border and training is going really well.

'I think we will run well under 2:08 and possibly close to 2:07. But I'm not imposing any limits on myself. If I've gone through the half in 63 and I'm feeling comfortable then I am not going to deliberately slow down. There's no point in placing limits on yourself. It could be anything.'

Rob had a special private source of motivation to tap. Gayelene had telephoned him from Australia to confirm that she was pregnant.

Gayelene remembers, 'He was very excited. He told me: "I am really particularly missing you now. It's a beautiful time and we should be spending it together. I think it is something that will bring us even closer together, if that is possible."

'He is so positive about it and is such a gentle person. I know he will be an exceptionally good father. He won't just stand off all day and then put the child to bed as so many do.'

Gayelene was soon on her way to join Rob and her brother in Bergen-Dal. When Ron Clarke heard their news he predicted it would have a bearing on the race. 'Some men are not greatly affected by fatherhood but, knowing Rob, I'm sure he will feel intensely about it. I think it will give him quite a lift.'

Salazar, accompanied by a burly Finnish masseur, booked into the hotel six days before the race and joined the de Castella group for dinner on his first night there. Rob liked him. 'Alberto is a nice, easy-going guy and I enjoy his company. I think the media sometimes creates a personality for people like him which is only distantly related in reality.'

In the flesh, Salazar certainly looked a man apart from some of his press interviews. There was an air of boyish vulnerability about him as he survived some painfully ill-informed interviews by non-specialist Dutch journalists. One reporter opened a conversation by asking him his best time for the marathon. The big Latin eyes flashed impatiently but the replies were always measured and courteous.

The lack of tension between Rob and Alberto was illustrated when they warmed up together for a track session four days before the race and, after doing their individual workouts, warmed down together. The American's masseur, Ilpo, went to work on the Australian's leg and back muscles in the week before the race, and he also did his best to ease calf problems dogging Graham Clews.

A few days before the race, the organizers hired a bus to drive some of the top runners around the course. Rob recalled, 'Alberto kept asking the driver, "Are we coming to the finish? Where's the finish line? Are we getting close to the finish?" I thought to myself, "Settle down a bit, Alberto." Then, when we finally got there, he suddenly jumped from his seat behind me and dipped his chest past me, shouting, "Gotcha!"

'When I got over the surprise and stopped laughing, I said, "You kicked too early. The race isn't for two days."

'Alberto replied, "Well, that's a change. I'm usually too late."

'You couldn't help liking somebody who kept his sense of humour during the build-up to a race like that.'

After the bus ride the runners faced a battery of journalists in a magnificent lord mayoral chamber in Rotterdam's City Hall. The main contenders all agreed a world record was a distinct possibility and a halfway split of around 64 would be ideal. Rob and Salazar both told questioners that as far as they were concerned the winner would be entitled to call himself the world's best marathoner, at least until they had a rematch.

Later, at a less formal gathering, Salazar gave an assurance that he didn't expect Rob to make all the pace, as he had in shorter races like Gasparilla. 'We haven't made any plans to share the pace-setting, but I'm ready to do my bit,' he said.

The tactical pattern of the race was irrevocably altered when Pat Clohessy hit town. The wily coach had a run over the vital last 10 km of the course, noting three rises which were the nearest things to hills in table-flat Rotterdam, and then went to talk to Rob. 'I advised him to be very careful about the pace and all this talk of a world record. He should just stay relaxed and make sure he is in contact. The time will work itself out. He just has to run to win.'

Noting the nature of the course and the rapidly improving weather, Clohessy shook his head in wonder at the possibilities. 'They could run anything, anything,' he said.

He told Rob he would like to see him run a race similar to the Brisbane gold medal effort, staying relaxed and then accelerating in the final 10 km. Clohessy was firm about the tactics. 'He has to be wary of throwing everything into one burst and then not being able to maintain his drive to the finish. It's essential that when he goes, he goes all the way. If Salazar starts surging he will just relax off the pace a bit. Let him take twenty or thirty seconds and just keep running at a steady pace. It will soon close up. If he does that he is running his own race, not the race Salazar wants him to run. If they go through the halfway in sixty-three minutes that might not be unreasonably fast. It depends how he feels on the day.

'But there are a lot of good runners in this field and if Rob and Alberto get too carried away, they face the danger of knocking each other out and then being beaten by someone who has run a more cautious race.'

The Institute of Sport had flown Clohessy around the world to be with his star pupil on the big day, so the Australians planned a gesture of gratitude. They cut an institute logo from a souvenir pennant Clohessy had brought along and Gayelene stitched it to the blue-and-white striped singlet Rob was to wear in the race.

Clohessy was anxious that Rob should not have to take the lead too early, so he suggested to Rich Castro, the coach of the two Gomezes, that Rodolfo's best hope of victory rested with a solid pace over the final 16 km. He nodded in quiet satisfaction when Castro conceded that he probably was right.

Everything was ready.

Start to 5 km

The gun propelled them from the shadow of Rotterdam's imposing Gothic city hall. Light planes circled over, trailing banners which read 'Succes Gerard Nijboer', 'Succes Alberto Salazar' and 'Succes Robert de Castella'. Coolsingel, the wide, fashionable main shopping street, was packed with appreciative fans as Salazar moved straight up to share the lead with the Scot John Graham, a last-minute entry. Rob followed his rival forward and positioned himself discreetly behind the Scot. As they negotiated a gentle rise past a quay lined with river barges, all varnish and brass in the sunshine, the three leaders were joined by the balding Hispanic-looking Rodolfo Gomez, his stocky Amerindian compatriot Jose Gomez, Carlos Lopes and Armand Parmentier. When they swung left across a bridge to run down a broad boulevard flanking the Rhine Estuary, the Dutchmen Nijboer and Lambregts closed up to complete the leading pack.

There was little more than a gentle breeze along the river bank where the field is more exposed to the weather than on any other part of the course. The temperature was about 10° C and the humidity around 70 per cent. Rodolfo Gomez and Graham led eight men in Indian file past the 5 km point in 15:02.

5 km to 10 km

They climbed a little slope to a traffic over-pass before swinging left away from the river along a wide avenue, Kralingse Zoom, which would take them to the three loops around Kralingse Lake that made up two-thirds of the race. Rob accepted a sponge at the 8 km but Salazar declined while Graham and Gomez opened a little break. Graham glanced back at the others and slowed when he saw they were in no hurry to catch him. Nijboer wasn't finding things easy. His left hamstring began to cramp, apparently because of a change in his running posture brought about by a numb feeling in his right calf where he had been bitten by a dog a few days previously. He dropped off the leaders' pace and asked his trainer to call a doctor. When no medico could be found the European champion decided to struggle on, to keep faith with his supporters in the crowd. He eventually finished fifteenth in 2:25:23. The remaining seven front-runners continued through avenues of bare, winter-stricken trees to a drinks table about halfway around the first loop. Rob drank, as he had at 5 km, but Salazar passed up the chance for a second time, although TV close-ups soon showed him licking his lips, as if his mouth was dry. The 10 km came up in 30:21.

10 km to 15 km

As the leaders swung to their left around the lake, Rob moved to the front, giving Graham a respite. The Commonwealth champion looked strong and relaxed as he strode over some rather uneven brick paving. This was a beautiful part of the run, with a perfectly restored mediaeval windmill reflected in the still waters on the far side of the lake. But even if the runners had been interested in such distractions, the scenery was masked by lines of shouting spectators and a cavalcade of pedallers matching the leaders' pace on a cycle track paralleling the roadway. There was now a substantial gap between the eight leaders and the second pack, which included Clews, Nijboer and a remarkable 52-year-old Dutchman, Piet van Alphen.

Up front, John Graham was back in the lead as they began the first of the race's two longer loops and he passed 15 km in 45:32, on schedule for a 2:08:00. Rob was glancing about and looking remarkably composed despite the cyclists and roller skaters 'buzzing' the athletes. One of the race organizers became so angry at the cyclists' antics he leaned from an official car to deliver a stiff-arm tackle, but broke his own arm. A member of Nijboer's support team had a more successful encounter when he despatched a rider, complete with bike, into the greenish water of a canal. At the time the weather was better for cycling than for swimming. Amid all this mayhem, the leaders' pace slackened a little.

15 km to 20 km

Jos Hermens, eager to see Rotterdam become the scene of history's first 2:07 marathon, jumped from one of the official vehicles and ran beside Graham, urging him to pick up the pace still further. The Scot looked annoyed. He had already tried to lift the tempo once, only to find the others reluctant to follow. Now Graham brushed aside an over-enthusiastic sponge dispenser and put his head down as the road swung left past some desolate high-rise blocks and further hordes of cyclists. But once again the others elected to let him go. He looked over his shoulder, saw the growing gap and slowed again. The competitive Scot looked distinctly uncomfortable in his rabbit role. When he led them past the 20 km marker in 61 minutes, after a 5 km split of 15:28, the hopes of a world record had slipped alarmingly. Lambregts had quietly dropped away from the leading group.

20 km to 25 km

Salazar now moved up to second place, took a drink and offered it around after taking a mouthful. Rob felt at this stage that the pace was a shade slow, but in keeping with Clohessy's advice, he held himself back. He said: 'I don't know how the others were finding it, but I felt comfortable. A bit too comfortable, in fact.'

Graham took them to the halfway in 1:04:26, promptly stepped from the road and clapped his erstwhile companions on their way. Salazar took over and Rob moved quickly to his shoulder. As they circled the lake for a second time, the race — despite all the world record predictions — had developed into a tactical stalemate. The six remaining leaders were all waiting for somebody else to throw down his cards.

Rob's feet were blistering, toenails on each foot were lifting and he felt the onset of diarrhoea. Yet he still looked relaxed and as nerveless as a gunslinger. Rodolfo Gomez had the beginnings of huge blood blisters on either foot and Parmentier was showing signs of weakening, drifting back a little when the pace picked up but closing again when the leaders eased. Little Carlos Lopes ran smoothly, as he had for almost 25 km, toward the back of the leading group and wide enough to be clear of any jostling. His relaxed, high-armed rhythm evoked memories of Juma Ikangaa. A 5 km split in 15:23 brought them to the 25 km point, with Rob leading a compact bunch in 1:16:23, about a 2:09 schedule. The Australian tossed his sponge at least fifteen metres straight into a bucket, then laughed as he boasted about his accuracy to Rodolfo Gomez.

25 km to 30 km

Salazar took the lead as Rob ran into a stomach crisis. The Australian said: 'I was getting pain and I just had to let it go.'

He drifted back 20 m as he cleaned himself with a sponge and his misadventure had a humorous spin-off in the Canberra Marathon a few hours later on the other side of the world. A Sydney runner, Doug Martin, said, 'We saw Deek rubbing the backs of his legs with a sponge during the TV coverage of the race. The English commentators said something about him knowing his body so well because he was a biophysicist and that he must be cooling down vital muscles. That was good enough for me. At every sponge station in Canberra I wiped down my hamstrings and I noticed that runners all around me were doing the same.'

If only they had known.

The other leaders let a tactical lottery win pass them by when none was willing to make a decisive move during the Australian's few minutes of inconvenience. Rob was back with the pack by the time Rodolfo Gomez went to the front in what appeared to be his long-awaited tactical thrust. But Rob observed, 'He took the lead, but that was all. He didn't do anything. It's no good just going there, you have to do something.'

Salazar soon repassed the Mexican and led the pack past the 30 km point in 1:31:47, after a split of 15:24.

30 km to 35 km

The tension was becoming cruel. Somebody just had to make a move. Back at the press centre overlooking the start–finish, Gayelene, fearing that Rob was leaving his run too late and might be over-whelmed in a sprint finish, said: 'Robert will have to do something soon.'

Ron Clarke, who had flown from London where he was on a business visit, was reassuring. 'It's OK. He's looking really good.'

On the course, Clohessy, who was perched on top of the coaches' truck following the runners, felt gnawing responsibilities for the race plan he had urged for Rob's day of truth. What if it simply left him exposed to finishers with more basic speed?

But Rob, over his stomach upset, was actually laughing his head off. He explained, 'When you are out there running behind the photographers' truck, you get sick and tired of them pointing their cameras and firing flash bulbs into your face. They look so smug and comfortable. When you are very tired you even start to hate them a bit. So it seemed hilarious to us when one of them dropped a huge lens from the truck and it went tinkle, tinkle, all over the road. I couldn't stop laughing.'

The six runners completed their final circuit of the lake with Rodolfo Gomez back in the lead and reached 35 km in 1:47:43, having run the last 5 km in 15:56, easily the slowest split of the race. Yet they still waited. Rob said, 'I think they all assumed that I was the one to take the lead because I was the slowest 10 km runner in the leading bunch. I knew if I did everyone else would sit back and let me do all the work.'

Hopes of a world record were gone — the expectation now was more like 2:10 — but the tactical situation was riveting.

35 km to 40 km

Rob, with a best 10,000 m time of 28:12:2, now faced a contest over

7.2 km with track aces Salazar (27:25:61) and Lopes (27:24:39). 'Have faith in your finish,' Clohessy had counselled him. 'It's strength that counts at the end of a marathon and you're stronger than any of them.'

The runners, with Rodolfo Gomez beginning at last to stride out determinedly, swung past a little group of Australians with an improvised banner saying 'Go Deek' and ran on to Kralingse Zoom to begin the race to the finish. Jose Gomez dropped back, but the tenacious Parmentier still clung on.

On a slight upgrade, not worthy of the word 'hill' but still one of the most noticeable rises on the course, Deek decided to go. The strain immediately showed on the faces of the other survivors as he poured on the power. He crested the rise, led the way down a short slope off Kralingse Zoom, then dug in even harder on another upgrade. As he surged up the second hill, Salazar simply dropped away. He was beaten! The world record-holder said, 'I felt fine until that point, then when Robert picked it up I just started to lose ground. I tried but I just couldn't pull him back.'

Rob didn't realize he had disposed so easily of his previously unbeaten arch-rival. He said, 'I hoped they would think I was merely surging. But once I went, there was no way I was going to slow down until the finish.'

As Parmentier lost contact and the gap to Salazar widened to forty metres, Clohessy almost tumbled from the top of the truck in his excitement. Just after 37 km Gomez, who had been running with a near-sprint action just to keep up, had to let go. Rob said, 'I expected to have Alberto and the others right behind me, but when I looked back I saw only Carlos and I knew it would be a fast finish.'

As Rob drove powerfully along a narrow cobbled street with a dyke towering on one side and cafés and shops on the other, Lopes looked so comfortable he was obviously now a major factor in the race.

An official vehicle had driven into the gap behind the Portuguese. Rob reminded himself that Salazar could be lurking right behind the truck ready to surprise him at the finish. He kept accelerating, running each kilometre faster than the previous one and tore past 40 km in 2:02:21, having covered 5 km in 14:38.

40 km to Finish

Despite this fastest eighth 5 km in the history of world-class marathoning, the little Portuguese was still at Rob's shoulder and still looked controlled and dangerous.

In the press centre Gayelene sat immobilized. Asked if the marathoner could possibly beat the track speedster over the final 2.2 km, Clarke replied, 'I don't know. Strength is vital. I think so. But you can never tell.'

Rob was wary. 'I knew very well that Carlos was an excellent track runner. His 10,000 m best is nearly a minute faster than mine, but at the end of a marathon it isn't the same thing. I didn't want to be surprised so I started to test him a little after the fortieth kilometre, seeing if I could put some fatigue into his legs. But surprise! He was able to follow me very easily.'

Rob slowed briefly to see how Lopes would react, but the Portuguese just slowed with him.

So the pace was soon on again, and down to 4:38 mile tempo as the two men raced together back towards the massed crowds on Coolsingel. With about 600 m to go the Portuguese seemed to edge a body thickness ahead. Gayelene whispered fearfully: 'He's going past.'

Rob, his eyes fixed grimly ahead, dug for even more speed. He said: 'With 500 to go, I just put my head down and ran as hard as I could. Almost a sprint.'

His arms pumped, his knees lifted like a sprinter's and he proved Clohessy right. Over that final half a kilometre, strength gradually, painfully asserted itself over speed and a tiny, re-won advantage became a winning margin. Rob stormed over the finish line two seconds clear to win one of history's great marathon contests in 2:08:37. He had run the final 2.2 km in an amazing 6:16, the final 400 m in about sixty seconds and his race time had been bettered only by Salazar, himself and Derek Clayton.

Clohessy said: 'We worked out our race plan and Rob executed it brilliantly ... this gives him a tremendous mental advantage in the future. He did everything as planned, kept his cool, and won the race like a champion.'

Rob, who had now won from the front in Fukuoka, from behind in Brisbane and with a late, controlled kick in Rotterdam, was jubilant. 'I really wanted to show them that strength can win over speed. I'm sure a lot of these guys are going to have to go back and have another look at their training and their race strategies.'

Lopes' 2:08:39 was a new European record and made him the fifth fastest in the history of the event.

Rodolfo Gomez was third in 2:09:25 and announced he would, henceforth, follow Rob's example and race much more sparingly than his recent six marathons in thirteen months.

Parmentier was fourth in 2:09:56, a Belgian record, and Salazar fifth in 2:10:08, the slowest of his five marathons but the fastest time run by an American outside the US. Surprisingly, it was also an American record for an out-and-back or loop course. The dethroned king told the after-race press conference: 'I guess I just wasn't mentally prepared. I had begun to believe the things a few of you guys had written about me being unbeatable. I wasn't hungry enough.'

Later, in an interview with *Track & Field News*, he referred to the groin strain. 'When I made my decision to come, I wasn't at 100 per cent. But I felt the leg was as good as at other times when I wasn't 100 per cent. Plus I feel if you are a champion, you can run and win when everything isn't going perfectly. If I was to have chickened out, it would have hurt me more in the long run than if I ran badly and got beaten. I won't have nightmares about it. Once you start doubting yourself, you don't know where it is going to stop.'

Jose Gomez was sixth in a PB 2:12:27, Lambregts was seventh in 2:12:40, Peter Russman (Holland) eighth in 2:16:23 and Graham Clews ninth in 2:17:00, a personal best achieved despite pre-race calf muscle problems and severe cramps which forced him to drop to a walk several times in the final kilometres.

Piet van Alphen set a world record for the 50–55 age group when he finished fourteenth in 2:22:14 and Rosa Mota of Portugal was the first female home in a personal best of 2:32:27.

CHAPTER SEVENTEEN

On Top Of The World

The Rotterdam victory confirmed Rob as a national hero in Australia and sharply increased his value on the international running market. He arrived home to a wide range of endorsement offers and some financially tempting race invitations, headed by a determined bid, supported by IMG in the US, to have him contest the New York Marathon instead of, or after, the World Championships in Helsinki. The respite between Rotterdam and Helsinki, little more than three months, was the shortest gap he had faced between major marathons. Clohessy bristled at the idea of having him run another gruelling event in October only a further two months after the World Championships. The race director of the New York Marathon, Fred Lebow, said this of the Australian: 'De Castella could earn more money, above and below the table, than any other athlete in the world if he ran in America. He would be the highest paid runner on earth, getting more than the milers and more than Carl Lewis.' Lebow, often described as the father of the running boom, thought de Castella could probably earn $500,000 by running one marathon and seven or eight other races in the US before the Olympics.

However, Rob and Clohessy had set their targets years before and were not to be deflected. Rob stated, 'People who chase dollars don't win the major titles. It does not fit in with my long-term goals to run another marathon before the Olympics. I will go to the World Cross-country Championships in New York in March and also probably run some shorter road races in the US next year.'

Despite keeping athletic success as his major priority, there could be no doubt Rob was finding dollars a little easier to come by. There was $12,500 from Rotterdam in his trust account with the AAU and more was to follow after the signing of a two-year endorsement contract with a health food distributor, Calorie Control Foods. Other similar deals were under consideration and advertisements featuring the Deek running style in partnership with various products were appearing with increasing frequency in magazines, newspapers and on TV. He took part in a variety of promotional press conferences and was guest TV commentator at the inaugural Wang-sponsored Australian Marathon. The trust fund was soon swelling past the $150,000 mark.

The weekly training routine had expanded to include nearly 220 km of running, five sessions in the gymnasium, two sessions in the swimming pool and two massages which he had come to regard as beneficial following his encounters with Salazar's friend Ilpo in Berg-en-Dal. This left him not more than two hours a day for other activities, so his position at the Institute of Sport had been modified to Special Projects Director. He will grin and not disagree if you suggest that the special projects are gold medals.

He told Brian Lenton in *Through The Tape* how he judged the torrent of demands he received on his time. 'The first test is whether the invitation will adversely affect my training or preparation for competition. It must pass that test before I'll do anything. The next thing is that I prefer to encourage and try to motivate kids to participate in sporting activities. I will always go to a school or junior presentation night before doing something for the adult community. The other consideration is financial. If I feel that something is going to be financially worthwhile then I will seriously consider it, providing it fits in with the first prerequisite.'

The prerequisite was preparing in the Stromlo Forest, following his encouragingly quick recovery from Rotterdam, for the next big challenge.

The event before the Big One brings the greatest difficulties in mental preparation. No matter how often you tell yourself the immediate challenge is the only one that matters, it's hard to keep a looming major event out of your subconscious, to prevent yourself from conserving just a bit of commitment for it. Such subconscious checks have been at the root of many a sporting disaster. For a less mentally strong athlete than Rob, the marathon at the inaugural World Track and Field Championships on 15 August 1983 would have been fraught with danger, coming as it did soon after his Rotterdam triumph but before the Big One, the 1984 Olympic race. It was his third top-level marathon in ten months and he suffered an unsettling injury just before it, yet he was obviously less apprehensive than many of his rivals.

Salazar had opted for the Helsinki 10,000 m months before Rotterdam and not long after that race the four top Japanese, the Sohs, Seko and Itoh, confirmed they were out of the marathon running. They said they preferred to concentrate on their national trial at Fukuoka later in the year. A rash of scratchings followed. The US trial winner Grey Meyer said he preferred the 10,000 m and then dropped out with injury anyway. Rodolfo Gomez, Jose Gomez and Gidamis Shahanga all opted for the 10,000 m. Carlos Lopes, after some sparkling track performances, said he would try for the double, but he withdrew from the marathon after a disappointing run in the Helsinki 10,000 m. Salazar, whose post-Rotterdam motivation had out-stripped his physical recovery, also fared badly in the long track race.

Rob had no doubts about his own commitment to the event. 'This is a world championship. It ranks in importance close to or equal with the Olympics. Anybody wanting to be regarded as the world's best should be here.'

The obvious challengers in a big field included Commonwealth silver medallist Juma Ikangaa, in-form American Ron Tabb and the dual Olympic champion Waldemar Cierpinski, who had shown good recent form in winning the inaugural European Nation's Cup team marathon. There were a dozen other runners who could not be dismissed.

Rob's preparation had progressed smoothly but unspectacularly. Before leaving Australia he ran an impressive 10 mile (16 km) road race in Melbourne in 46:33. Then during a London stopover with the rest of the Australian team, he nudged eight minutes for 3,000 m at the Talbot Games and ran fourth in the 10,000 m at the British championships, clocking 28:17. He had hoped to finally crack twenty-eight minutes in the longer run, but said afterwards, 'I don't think that was a negative indicator for my marathon form. I have been in heavy training and the weather has been unusually hot in Britain. I went into the race feeling a bit tired and the way it evolved tactically meant that fast times were not on.'

After the British titles, Rob moved right out of the spotlight, flying to Oslo to stay in a holiday apartment organized by the great Norwegian runner Grete Waitz and her husband Jack. Rob had formed a friendship with Waitz during trips to the US and the World Cross-country Championships and the Norwegian had paid him a compliment he valued above most others. After her 15 km world best in Tampa, Florida, Waitz was fielding questions at a post-race gathering and was asked which male athlete she most admired. She replied that she had not been asked that question before, had not given it any thought, but she sought out Rob later and told him: 'If I had had time to think about it I would have answered "Robert de Castella." '

Waitz is noted for the intensity of her training and Rob has had some influence on moderating her workouts. When they ran together in the US, she found the pace was slower than she usually adopted when she was alone and this impressed her. She had thought of long, slow running as boring and usually had run as hard as she could to get through her longer workouts as quickly as possible. After training with Rob, she realized it was unnecessary to thrash her body to maintain an already superb level of fitness. As Rob pointed out, she could reduce the frequency of leg injuries by doing long runs at a more relaxed pace. Now the Australian ran with Waitz through the conifer and silver beech forests outside the Norwegian capital while Gayelene and Jack Waitz checked their watches and joked about the length of their spouses' absences. The two runners obviously found each other's company beneficial. On the opening day of competition in Finland, Grete ran away from the women's marathon field in scorching weather to win the first gold medal in track and field's first World Championship.

Rob remained in Oslo, paying only a flying visit to Helsinki's hurly-burly to look over the course, noting its many sharp hills, particularly a big one between 37 km and 39 km, and the way it was exposed for much of its course to winds off the Baltic Sea. He discussed the tactical ramifications with Clohessy and the coach once again urged him to hold back and have faith in his finishing ability.

The 10,000 m final had given Clohessy some ideal motivational material. He reminded Rob that he had dominated Cinque Mulini four months earlier, beating Alberto Cova, Werner Schildhauer and Hans-Jorge Kunze. The same three men won the medals in a tight finish in the long track race in Helsinki.

Three days before the marathon, Rob had a frightening mishap which left him hobbling. Would he be able to run on Sunday? Would it be the kind of injury that is fine for 20 km and then becomes a major problem in the late stages of a marathon? Would it lead to crippling cramps or simply fold up on that big hill 5 km from home?

Rob explained the accident like this. 'I was getting a twinge of sciatica in the lower back and upper buttocks. Strangely, this seems to occur whenever I ease back my training. I'm not sure why. There was no automatic traction machine in the Games Village so I had to settle for an inversion table which I had read about, but hadn't used before. I decided to take the risk of using unfamiliar treatment, which I suppose wasn't the wisest course just a few days before a World Championship. So I got on the table and stretched my back and it seemed to loosen a bit. The problem was that I came up sore in the upper left thigh the next day. It hurt me to walk, particularly up or down stairs. I had tapered off my training so I wasn't sure whether it was going to affect my running or not, but we were really concerned. I considered withdrawing and adjusting my programme to a race two months later in the New York Marathon. We didn't know at the time that the whole TV hook-up from Australia was dependent on my competing. The one hope was that since I didn't suffer the injury running, perhaps running wouldn't aggravate it. I had physiotherapy and treated it myself with ice packs and so forth. There was the worry that it might stir up during the marathon and become a major problem and I was aware I might have to quit during the race.'

In line with Rob's no-excuses philosophy, the press did not learn the details of the injury and once again he demonstrated his ability to handle even the most intense mental pressure. He recalled Salazar's statement that a true champion could compete and win even when he was not 100 per cent and remembered Salazar's fate in Rotterdam when he tried to put that belief into practice while still recovering from a muscle injury. Another athlete might have buckled under the mental pressure, but Rob is no ordinary competitor. He said, 'I had to avoid getting emotionally caught up in the possibilities. Looking back at the incident later it seems that I could easily have let it upset me, but when you are keyed up for a big race you seem to have a capacity to accept these things. You adopt an attitude of what will be will be, and I think that's the only way to handle it. It's no good getting upset and up-tight about something you have no control over. I recalled something I had read in one of Lasse Viren's books. After he won the 10,000 m in the Munich Olympics in 1972 he did a victory lap holding his shoes above his head and was hauled over the coals by the officials and threatened with disqualification from the 5,000 m. This was all happening on the night before the heats, but he said: "It was no good me worrying about it. I had the Finnish team manager and the coach to sort out the problem for me and the best thing I could do was avoid getting emotionally involved and just continue to prepare myself for the race. If I was not allowed to run, then it would be bad luck, but if they allowed me to run it was my responsibility to be in as good shape as I could." I tried to take a leaf from Viren's book.'

The marathon started in the middle of the afternoon on the last day of competition. The weather had cooled suddenly and a strong wind was gusting from the sea as eighty-two runners circled the Olympic stadium and then streamed out on to the loop course straddling the isthmuses and islands of the port's suburbs. They went down a steep hill in the first few kilometres and Rob felt an alarming pain in his thigh. He said, 'The physio had warned me the injury was most likely to hurt on a down grade. So I just hoped I wouldn't feel it again. As it warmed up it stopped worrying me.'

Like a commuter trying to keep balance in the rush hour charge, he adjusted to the pace of those ahead and behind him in a huge forty-runner pack. The first 10 km was covered in a cautious 31:25 and various athletes, including Ikangaa and his fellow Tanzanian Agapius Masong, Tabb and the Italians Marco Marchai and Gianpaolo Messina, took a turn in front. Surprisingly, Ikangaa showed no inclination to bolt away as he had in Brisbane and again in the Tokyo Marathon earlier in the year. Instead, he had a glance at Rob and tucked himself into the throng, not too far from the Australian.

None of the leaders pushed hard enough to scatter the pack. Rob said: 'The first part of the race was pretty quiet. I was just trying to conserve energy and the only thing that worried me was the jostling. It was a bit hard to stay on your feet.'

The 15 km passed in 46:44 after a 5 km split of 15:19. Rob recalled, 'This was relatively fast and I was amazed at how many runners were still up there. It seemed everybody else was sitting back watching me and waiting for me to make a move. In a way I was dominating the situation tactically, because they were all running at a pace that suited me. This was accentuated by the nature of the course. Nobody wanted to go out and push too early over all those undulating hills. With the wind so strong at various stages, it also made sense that many runners were looking for a nice sheltered place at the back of the pack where they could relax.'

Cierpinski, as was his tactical habit, avoided the spotlight early in the race, appearing alert and animated only when Rob seemed about to make a move. But one of the lessons the Australian had learned years earlier from the formidable East German was that marathon winners don't show their cards too early. Rob said, 'I was very aware Cierpinski was running well. Our Italian friend, Dr Rosa, had warned me that Cierpinski's European results indicated he was in good shape and you have to respect him because of his unbelievable history in major championships. I spent a lot of the Moscow Marathon running beside or just behind him and I learned a lot there about self-control and tactics. He is a master tactician.'

The 21.1 km came up just after 1:05, a comparative dawdle, but Rob said, 'It was an uncomfortable race as there were so many hills and turns. Runners were constantly clipping your heels or you were clipping theirs. A couple of the Italians fell, I think.'

Pier Giovanni Poli, one of the two to go sprawling just past the halfway, recovered gamely to finish seventh in a new Italian record.

The 25 km went by in 1:17:59 (31:06 for 10 km) and then, for the first time, Rob was presented with a serious tactical decision. Masong, tall and slightly stooped, took off suddenly over one of the wind-swept bridges with Kebede Balcha of Ethiopia and Robleh ('Flannel') Djama of Djibouti chasing him. Rob stayed in the pack and as the gap behind the three Africans stretched to about fifty metres, Gayelene, who had become a TV commentator for the day, confessed to Australian audiences that she was getting a trifle worried.

Rob was confident. 'From about 37 km, the course swung around and we would have a tailwind. I didn't want to go to the front a long way before that and have to lead into a headwind. The wind and the hill at 37 km made that the breaking point for my competitors.

Ideally, I wanted to be in the lead just a bit before so I could pick up the pace and ensure they were running close to their thresholds before I put the pressure on up the hill.'

His decision not to chase the Africans was vindicated 2 km later when Masong eased back and Djama was left a reluctant leader. By 30 km, reached in 1:33:10, Tabb had towed a pack of about seventeen runners up to the breakaway Africans. At this point the pace was lagging nearly 1:30 behind Rotterdam's tempo and Rob's supporters began to get jumpy. How slowly could he afford to let the race be run before his opponents' speed became more potent than his own strength?

The waiting ended abruptly after 33 km when the red-headed Briton Hugh Jones rushed to the front and quickly strung the remaining leaders into Indian file. Rob was satisfied. 'I was relieved when Hugh committed himself to a course of action. Before that there were so many guys playing cat-and-mouse with each other that you were not sure how the race would unfold. When he went, the race changed dramatically into a tactical contest rather than a situation where a lot of guys were just running along together at a pretty fair clip.'

Rob reacted quickly to the new situation, passing Jones and breaking free with remarkable ease. Only little Balcha stayed at his shoulder. Rob said, 'Once we got the tailwind I went. What surprised me was how quickly the others dropped off. All at once there were just two of us and I could see that Kebede was running easily up the smaller hills. I had sprinted over the top of him once before, at Stramilano, and was confident I could do the same again if need be.'

Ikangaa, who had seemed indecisive in his new role as follower rather than leader, was beaten by this stage, a victim, Rob suspects, of the pressures of his new environment at a US university. The Swede Kjell-Erik Stahl led a group including Cierpinski and Belgium's Armand Parmentier, but they were soon 20 m in arrears and the gap was growing.

Rob, experienced by now in the art of shaking off shadows, had only Balcha to worry about. 'I deliberately upped the pace on the big hill to test him. That was where I got away from him. But I must say I was relieved when I opened up that final gap on him. Once I had the gap I just concentrated on working it up and being really controlled. I knew then that all I had to do was maintain my form and rhythm.'

The Australian's ability to *kick-down* — increasing the pace so sharply his opponents could not respond — had put him within reach of his fourth successive major marathon. He ran alone past 40 km in 2:03:28, after a 10 km split of 30:18 and a kilometre following steep hills in 2:53. His thigh held up but with 2 km to go his face was showing the strain. Then he heard Clohessy shouting from the side of the road that he had a 100 m lead. 'I felt more relaxed from there on in,' he said.

Despite this easing of the competition and the effects of Helsinki's cruelly placed hills, he covered the final 2.2 km in 6:31 which compared surprisingly well with that desperate 6:16 in Rotterdam.

He circled the Olympic Stadium track to a thunderstorm of applause and allowed himself a relieved salute as he neared the tape. He recalled, 'Once I was inside the stadium I just indulged in the emotion and satisfaction of taking out my first World Championship.'

He finished in 2:10:03 to formalize the title he had earned in Rotterdam: Marathon Champion of the World.

Balcha held on to take the silver medal comfortably in 2:10:27 while Cierpinski overhauled Stahl inside the stadium to snatch the bronze in 2:10:37.

Other top placings were: Stahl 2:10:38; Masong 2:10:42; Parmentier 2:10:57; Poli 2:11:05; Jones 2:11:15; Karel Lismont (Belgium) 2:11:24; and Stig Husby (Norway) 2:11:29.

Ikangaa was 15th in 2:13:11, Tabb 18th in 2:13:38 and Australia's Jeff Coole 38th in 2:20:25. The third Australian, Grenville Wood, failed to finish.

Rob's competitive embers were still aglow when he met Australian journalist Mike Hurst in the post-race tumult. He told Hurst: 'I won it on the hills. I couldn't care less about the time. I think I can call myself the world champion, irrespective of who was in the field . . . if they had wanted to be world champion they should have been here. But there are still a few I want to get.'

Later, in a quieter moment, he told Len Johnson, who was in Helsinki to write rather than run, that the accumulated pressures of three big marathons had made Helsinki particularly difficult. He said: 'Before you run a marathon you have to be really hungry, almost craving for a hard race. I've run three marathons in the past 10 months, all very hard and very intense and under tremendous pressure. It's hard to come back and put it on the line again, time after time.'

Johnson's expert comments for the *Sydney Morning Herald* included a rebuttal of Canadian Jerome Drayton's prediction five years earlier that fast 10,000 m runners would soon dominate the marathon. Johnson wrote: 'Drayton's forecast was wrong...the major championships since have been won by Waldemar Cierpinski, Gerard Nijboer and Robert de Castella, none of whom has run the 10,000 m in under 28 minutes. It is the fast 10,000 m men such as Carlos Lopes and Alberto Salazar who have found out this year that they are incapable of utilizing that speed against de Castella at the finish.'

The World Champion's name had been written *Castella* on official handouts throughout the championships and when his gold medal was presented he found the *de* was also missing in the engraving. He returned the medal, evidence of the achievement of one of his greatest ambitions, to the organizers, saying, 'My name is not Robert Castella...I think they should get it right.' In the end, Rob took the original medal home, with a promise that a more accurate model would be forwarded to Canberra.

At the British championships, an English race caller had ockerised the runner's name to Bob Costella. These blunders recalled the days before international status when some Melbourne newspapers called him Robert de Costello. They don't get it wrong in Australia any more and it won't be long before the rest of the world is just as sure of the spelling.

CHAPTER EIGHTEEN

Ultimate Challenges

When nesting season arrives, Canberra's magpies are no respecters of reputations. Back home as World Champion and occasional luncheon companion to the Prime Minister, Bob Hawke, Rob met undisguised hostility along one of his regular training tracks, a ridge above the new split-level home he and Gayelene were renting and hoping to buy. Nesting magpies dive-bombed him so unmercifully he was forced to switch his shorter runs to the slightly more distant Stromlo Forest where there were only inoffensive rabbits and kangaroos along the tracks in the early morning. Otherwise it was good to be back in Canberra, which Rob and Clohessy had become convinced was the best distance running town in the world.

'There may be other places where the facilities are as good,' Rob believes, 'but you couldn't get better distance running paths than the ones we use in the Stromlo Forest [local runners had put up a sign designating one of the tracks Deek Drive] or a better sports-medicine back-up than the one at the Institute of Sport. Many other places are fine in summer but have unbearable weather in the winter and I don't know of anywhere else where there is as much co-operation and friendliness among the runners. We already have a very strong training group and this could be reinforced soon by the arrival of Gerard Barrett, which would follow the return of Dave Chettle from England. Some time in the future I will go to the States for an extended period of racing and perhaps to train at altitude, but I will always keep Australia as my base. I will always feel the need to come back here to settle into a routine of peace and quiet. Relaxation is a very important part of achieving your potential and it is easier to relax here than it is in the States where there are so many more distractions.'

Rob had come to consider Canberra a vital factor in re-establishing the routine that had taken him to the top of the world, the routine that Clohessy described as 'possibly the best in the world, or maybe the tenth best, but one that we know works'.

Rob said after Helsinki: 'I have to make sure I get back to the system I have been following for the past few years. I seem able to do that fairly easily and comfortably in Canberra. It's an environment that doesn't change and is free of distractions. It's a great help having Pat and Gayelene in such close proximity and they make it easy for me to slot back into the old routine.'

Rob had precisely defined his major ambition, leaving no ambiguity about his remaining goals. One was the Olympic gold medal at Los Angeles almost precisely a year after Helsinki; another was a world's best time for the marathon; and a third was the completion of his domination over all his rivals, with particular emphasis on a victory over Japan's Toshihiko Seko and another defeat of Alberto Salazar, because the Australian did not believe the world-record holder had been at his best in Rotterdam. After Rob had attended to these small matters, he reasoned, nobody in his right mind would be able to argue that he was not the greatest marathon runner in history.

He said, 'If the world record doesn't pop up in Los Angeles I would like to run New York because it is another potentially fast venue. There are enough fast marathon courses around to offer a fair choice for a world record attempt. I could possibly return to Rotterdam which is very fast. In a straight-out record attempt, I would like to have somebody set the pace for the first half or three-quarters of the race. I don't mind running, say, the last third, on my own but to be out in front much earlier than that can be very taxing mentally. The pace could be set by another competitor or, possibly, a pace-maker. Once the Olympics are over I won't feel I am under such intense pressure to defend my win–loss record against other runners. It would still be important but I will be more prepared to commit myself early in a race and accept the tactical risk that entails. When you talk about super-fast times you have to commit yourself very early and that makes you more vulnerable.

'I think 2:06 or 2:07 are possible but it would be very hard to push yourself if you were feeling exhausted and still had 15 or 20 km to go. You've got to have a lot of confidence in your fitness and strength, in your ability to hang together and keep on going. In a competitive situation you don't have any alternative. You have to stay with the competition to have any chance of winning but in a record attempt it is much easier to opt out and settle for a slower time. You have to have a lot of determination and faith in your own ability.

'The other thing I would like to achieve, aside from dominating my opposition and getting a world record, is to put the world record out of reach for a long period of time, as Derek Clayton did. I would like to establish a barrier that would defy other runners and be a challenge to them. People ask you what the ultimate marathon time is and what is the next barrier. They think of the four-minute mile and translate that into a two-hour marathon. That's a nice round figure but I think it's unrealistic. I think a more likely barrier would be one similar to Clayton's 1969 record of 2:08:34 which stood for so long it became like a four-minute mile barrier as far as the runners were concerned. I would like to establish a similar sort of mark which everybody else would try to chase.

'The thing I respect most about former distance greats is the way they pioneered new levels of performance. Ron Clarke completely changed the record book and runners like Dave Bedford and Brendan Foster also broke new ground, not only time-wise, but in the use of new tactics such as mid-race surges to throw off the opposition. These are things I respect distance runners for. They are the types of things I would still like to achieve. I may have established myself as number one, but I haven't given the sport back a single, definite achievement which would be remembered as helping in the development of distance running.'

Reminded that he had brought the marathon kick-down to a new level of intensity and would be remembered for the way he used it in Rotterdam and Helsinki, even if he didn't run another marathon, he conceded, 'Yes, I guess that is true.'

And after Los Angeles? 'I might concentrate a little more on establishing my financial security, but my priorities are not going to alter dramatically. There will be other goals that I will find just as worthwhile. I'm happy training and I get satisfaction from it and it's of long-term benefit from a health point of view, anyway. If anything, I would like to be able to increase the time I devote to running. Things might change if my other priorities and commitments begin to infringe on my training.

'I could see myself running marathons to 1988 and beyond and, if things work out that way, trying to win a second Olympic gold medal. As far as my age is concerned I think it is quite feasible. I will be 31 so there will be no physical problem. The unknown factor, at this stage, is my mental capability by that time, my hunger. It's impossible to predict. I'm as keen as I ever was to try hard to improve my performances and in the past I've gained a tremendous amount of motivation from my big races. LA could be a bigger boost than all the others. But I'm not sure what effect having a family will have on me and how it will affect my priorities. Gayelene and I hope it doesn't change things too much. We will just have to wait and see.'

Rob thought he would probably increase the frequency of his marathon racing after the Olympics, but stressed this would be no great departure from his routine. 'People say I only run one marathon a year but that has not always been true. In the past ten months I have run the Commonwealth Games, Rotterdam and the World Championships and when I first started running marathons I contested the Victorian title, the national, the Olympic trial and the Moscow Olympic race within a period of a little over eighteen months. I think this sort of intense programme can actually be beneficial. You have a period of intense competition which toughens you, but it is essential that you follow it with a more relaxed time where you can freshen up mentally and physically so you can come up for a big one. After Los Angeles I will probably follow a programme like that.

'As far as other road races in America are concerned, I would be quite flexible about distances and events. Most races there tend to range from 10 km to the half-marathon and possibly I will also visit Europe to run in some cross-country events as well as road races.

'I don't have any special ambition as far as world bests over the shorter road distances are concerned. I don't think a lot of these marks should be taken too seriously because the courses vary so much and can be downhill, wind-assisted and even short. I suppose it's illogical in a way, that marathon times remain so important to me and to other athletes since it is the longest race and therefore most vulnerable to these problems. In road running, the things that are most important are win–loss records and course records in the shorter events. The times are secondary, although it is obviously nice to pick up a world best.

'I don't know whether I would like to try to run the New York Marathon in 1984. It would be straight after the Olympics, perhaps a bit too close. But then a marathon in October 1985 would clash with the Commonwealth Games in early 1986. Depending how things evolve I would like to get in some good track running and try for the 10,000 m at the 1986 Commonwealth Games. It would be nice to defend my marathon title, but on the other hand I might find a fresh challenge more interesting. I sort of like the idea of having a try at the 10,000 m.'

Originally, the Australian's Olympic strategy included a stay of up to six months in the United States, but that idea was modified. He said, 'I will probably go over to the States about six weeks before the Games to train at Boulder or some other place where it is possible to have peace and quiet. I will just run and relax, getting used to the time zone and the warmer weather. I will probably have quite an entourage with me: Gayelene and Krista and somebody like Gayelene's mother to look after Krista while she is training and possibly Graham Clews to be my training partner.'

Geography and the commercial pressures of the so-called Free Enterprise Games promised to make the Olympic marathon especially testing. Because of the financial advantages of showing the marathon live at prime television viewing time in the United States, the start was scheduled for 5.15 p.m. when the Californian afternoon would still be hot and Los Angeles' notorious smog at its malodorous worst. High temperatures and atmospheric pollution would add to the physiological stress on the runners as they tackled the final quarter of the course, a gradual but steady climb for 10 km. It's a situation where only the strongest would prevail, so who could hope to challenge the world champion?

Rob believes Salazar and Seko are likely to play key roles in the race, particularly Salazar, who is a more motivated athlete following his Rotterdam setback. Hadn't Clohessy frequently pointed to the upsurges in performance following Rob's own rare defeats? Rob said, 'It is going to be tough for him because he is such an intense person and he trains so hard. I suspect he over-did his training after Rotterdam and he has to be careful not to fall into that trap again. I think he will come back because he has been through tough times before and got back on his feet and run well.'

As for Seko, who will be 28 in Los Angeles, Rob said, 'He is a most impressive athlete. He has speed and it is backed by good strength so he is able to use it at the end of a marathon. He seems very calm in a race and is a good tactician. I have run against him but I haven't really competed against him. I hadn't reached that level when he won the 1980 Fukuoka race and I finished eighth.'

Seko holds the world track records for 25,000 m (1:13:55.8) and 30,000 m (1:29:18.8), has run the marathon in 2:08:38 and hasn't been beaten in the event since losing to Bill Rodgers in 1979. He had been a national high school champion at 800 m and 1,500 m when he was accepted into the sporting family of the mystical coach Kiyoshi Nakamura who required him to crop his hair to symbolize his rejection of all personal desires, including sexual ones, and to fill his heart with *sanao* — the kind of unquestioning obedience which made it possible for Japanese pilots to crash their aircraft into Allied warships towards the end of the Second World War. Since accepting these conditions in 1977, Seko has lived with the Nakamuras, embracing the coach's philosophy of *zensoho* (running with Zen), and training fiercely as the master gradually adapted him, first to the 5,000 m and 10,000 m and then to the marathon. Seko won three consecutive Fukuokas — 1978, 1979 and 1980 — won the Boston Marathon in 1981 then was out of marathon action for two years before coming back brilliantly in 1983 to win the Tokyo Marathon in 2:08:38 and Fukuoka in 2:08:52. He denies suggestions by fellow Japanese that he is a robot programmed by Nakamura. He says, 'We follow Nakamura willingly because we know it is the right thing for us. We know he changes us, but we are aware of what's going on and we want it to happen. Love holds us together, not screws and bolts. The emotional support runners get from the Nakamuras and from each other is like that from a family.'

Nakamura has almost as many published thoughts as Chairman Mao, but just a few are enough to demonstrate the unusual nature of his relationship with his runners and its potential for providing Seko with spiritual fuel in Los Angeles. 'I am not God but I am his transmitter. These [the runners] are my children. When I preach to them stories about Jesus, the disciples, Buddha and the other great religious leaders, they believe them because they see me and they know people like that can exist ...

'I may tell my runners which path to take, but it is not my path, it is God's. I have so much power over my runners that I cannot afford to make a mistake. But I am human, so the only way I can be errorless is if I let God speak through me.'

Only Seko's long absences from top competition hang a question mark over his durability. When he isn't racing, the Nakamura camp tends to fob off journalists by saying he is too busy preparing for Los Angeles, but it has been reported that he has recurring problems with his right knee and he was treated in hospital for liver damage after the 1983 Tokyo Marathon. If he makes it to the Games fully fit, his confrontation with Rob will be worth the trans-Pacific air fare to see.

Seko's countrymen Takeshi and Shigeru Soh have spent most of their careers in his shadow, but the twins, who have a comparatively orthodox athletic background, have the credentials to make their presences felt in the big race. Takeshi has run 2:08:55 and Shigeru 2:09:06. During a 1983 visit to New Zealand, they set off for an ultra training run around Mount Egmont, with Shigeru covering 125 km in 8 hours and 26 minutes and Takeshi hanging in for 128.4 km in 8:37. That's the non-stop equivalent, in undulating country, of three successive marathons, each under 2:50. The run was a cornerstone of a build-up which the Sohs hope will bring them the world record, perhaps, they say, during the Los Angeles race.

Rob has beaten the Sohs, and all the others except Seko, but there are a few possible contenders he has yet to flatten over the marathon distance. Dual Olympic track champion Miruts Yifter (40 by Games time) was refused permission to run the marathon in Helsinki because he didn't have a qualifying time, but he has definite ambitions in the event and would be an interesting entry, as would New Zealander Rod Dixon, 33, who lacks marathon experience, but ran 2:08:59 to win the 1983 New York race and has boasted that he has the potential to run 2:05.

Despite Yifter's track and cross-country feats and Dixon's great record in shorter road races, Rob remained unimpressed. 'The potential for improvement of runners like Rod Dixon and Miruts Yifter is extremely limited. I don't think a lot of the good runners who might turn from shorter events to the marathon in LA will have been doing enough long running. Dixon, for example, doesn't do enough long runs to make much more of an impact on the marathon while Yifter has seen his best days. Both those runners have been competing for a long time and it's hard to see them marshalling enough mental freshness and determination for a winning Olympic performance. They no longer have the hunger.

'More likely challengers are Carlos Lopes, Rodolfo Gomez and possibly Greg Meyer. You have to expect some sort of special effort from the Americans because the race will be on their home soil where they always perform best. But a lot of the Americans lack the discipline needed to properly organize their racing programme. They get caught up chasing money or prestige and they race far too often. They neglect long-term goals.

'The marathon is a very difficult event to predict because the runners compete in so few of them. You can always get somebody coming along and improving dramatically, as I did at Fukuoka in 1981.'

He was well aware of those ambitious unknowns who come to the Olympics fired up for glory. Men like Abebe Bikila in 1960, Frank Shorter in 1972 and Waldemar Cierpinski in 1976.

'Possibly the World Championship victory will make it harder for me from a tactical point of view. There will obviously be a lot more expectation for me to perform and the opposition, having seen how a late kick-down has won the last two races for me, might try a different tactical approach. That doesn't concern me though. If they wait for me to make a move and then come with me, hoping to have something left at the finish, I will be in the same situation I was in at Rotterdam and Helsinki. If they decide to kick the pace up early, then I think that would suit me better from a competitive viewpoint. It's just that it is more demanding mentally to try to dominate a race from a long way out. It's a harder way to do it.

'The LA course is really quite fast and I think a world record is possible in the Olympic race, although I think it is unlikely. Julie Brown's front-running effort (2:26:24) there showed that fast times are possible. The things against a fast time are the conditions, likely to be warm and smoggy, and the way the race is likely to evolve tactically. If the Africans, say Balcha and Ikangaa, decide to dictate the tactics and make it a very fast pace during the early downhill stages then there will be a good chance of a world record, because you could find a situation where you just have to run a world record to win. Although the last 10 km are uphill, it's very gradual.'

Rob's performances in the past three years and his now proven ability to be ready on the big occasion, mean that any hopeful will have to produce a mighty marathon to topple him. How fast would you have to go to beat him from the front? I doubt that a 2:07:30 pace would shake him off. 2:07? 2:06:30? On the other hand, what sort of finishing drive would be good enough to outlast his kick-down in a sit-and-wait tactical race? He ran 6:16 for the final 2.2 km in Rotterdam and expects to improve before Los Angeles. He mused after his return to Australia, 'It will be the first time since before my 2:08:18 in Fukuoka that I have had a full year to prepare for a marathon. Last time I had the opportunity for that sort of preparation I improved by two and a half minutes . . .'

The long process of gradual adaptation has lifted Rob to a physiological plateau achieved by few other marathoners. His tenacity, courage and tactical skill complete a racing armoury probably unmatched in the history of the event. As Pat Clohessy said after the Rotterdam race: 'If they had finished over the top of him here they would have a strategy to use against him at the Olympics. But what do they do now?'